KATYE ANNA

VOLUME ONE

CONSCIOUS CONSTRUCTION OF THE SOUL

ANNA TEACHES HOW TO LIVE
A SOUL INSPIRED LIFE

CONSCIOUS CONSTRUCTION OF THE SOUL
Anna Teaches how to Live a Soul Inspired Life

Published by:
Transformation Books
211 Pauline Drive #513
York, PA 17402
www.TransformationBooks.com

ISBN: 978-0-9851407-8-6

Printed in the United States of America

A portion of the proceeds from the sale of this book will be donated to the charities the author supports.

VOLUME ONE

CONSCIOUS CONSTRUCTION OF THE SOUL

ANNA TEACHES HOW TO LIVE A SOUL INSPIRED LIFE

KATYE ANNA

DEDICATIONS

First and foremost I would like to thank Anna, she is the source of all the material in this book. I would also like to thank my soul partner and husband Allan for his support in helping me bring forth the teachings of Anna. I would also like to thank my family. My soul chose well when choosing each one of you. I want to thank my parents. My mother Kathryn Mummert continues to embrace that I am different. She doesn't understand much of what I teach but she supports my work and me. My dad David Nelson Mummert continues to encourage me from his own little place in heaven. My soul chose well when choosing to entrust my formative years to the souls known to me as my parents.

I also want to thank John Guy Baublitz III for his unconditional love and support while we journeyed together this lifetime. John continues to support me from the higher planes of consciousness within God. I miss John being in my physical life. I am blessed because I know he is with me and as John promised before he birthed into spirit we will never be separated.

I give a special thank-you to Christine Kloser. Christine was the first person Anna spoke to. Christine also has been a guide, and a major source of strength in getting our books published.

I want to thank my soul, spiritual teachers and guides, who journeyed with me on the many twists and turns of my life. Your patience, guidance, energy, teachings and love helped me to bring forth the creative expression of my soul. I am truly blessed. I used to be sad that I did not have teachers in physical bodies. I understand how blessed my life has been by having the angels lead me to my soul and my soul lead me to Anna. I have arrived. I am who I was born to be.

CONTENTS

Conscious Construction of the soul..................................2

Dedications..5

Preface 9

Chapter 1
The Beginning of Consciousness on Earth 15

Chapter Two
Creation beings on the Astral Planes............................23

Chapter Three
The Hall of Records and Soul Contracts 37

Chapter Four
The Earth Journey Begins 57

Chapter Five
Evolution of Souls through Experience

     Soul Parenting...72

Autism is Not a Condition.................................99

How Do We Help..110

Soul Energy Adjustment....................................131

Angels and Spirit Guides..................................136

Dreams and Astral Travel.................................149

The Seven Earth Planes of Consciousness....................157

Chapter 6
Samuel Reflects on His Life...............................177

Chapter 7
Elizabeth Moves into the Afterlife.....................205

Chapter 8
I Will be That Which You Need Me to Be.....................221

Authors Message 231

PREFACE

Conscious Construction of the Soul takes the reader on a journey of the incarnating soul. This is a journey we have all made many times. The journey begins on the astral plane of consciousness with a soul we will call Samuel, and moves through the process souls go through before incarnating on the physical plane we know as earth.

This book is written by an incarnated soul born in the year 1952. The incarnated soul was given the birth name of Katye Darlene Mummert. Around the earth year of 1988 after a soul re-alignment, Katye began the long road back to remembering the truth of her multidimensional beingness. Many shifts in consciousness were experienced by Katye. New doorways opened as Katye shifted. The remembrance of being an incarnated soul began to emerge. Although this book is not about Katye, it is about the experience of her soul and soul members of her family known as "Anna".

Katye: My journey into bringing forth the creative expression of my soul has not always been an easy one. There were many twists and turns on my path of bringing forth the voice and guidance of my soul, however, it has been an amazing journey.

When I was a little girl I always felt disconnected from those around me. My dad said I was "different" from his other children. Growing into a teenager who was "different" was not an easy path, however, it was my path. I realize now that my life with every twist and turn was orchestrated by the goals set forth by my soul for growth and soul expansion. Like many of you reading this, I was never taught by those around me that I was an incarnated soul. They, themselves, had long ago forgotten that they were incarnated souls. I was not taught that connecting with spirit guides, angels and traveling in consciousness to other planes of consciousness was normal.

Association with spirit guides and angels was normal for me as a child, but something I hid. I understand now that those around me could not hold space for my uniqueness. Like most families in the era I was born into, I was expected to fit into the established family instead of the family expanding, allowing me to find my own space. My soul chose a family who would teach me about love, and my parents did this well.

Today, as a 62 year old woman, I can see how the twists and turns of my life brought me to this place. I know I am an incarnated soul. I am here on this planet to learn, teach and embrace as much love as I can. I am here to teach that in God there is no separation between planes of consciousness. Consciousness itself or lack thereof is what determines how we experience our life.

My association with Anna, as well as the teachings from all my spiritual teachers and guides, has taken me on a journey of self discovery and growth. I haven't hidden for years that my guides and teachers are spiritual beings and that I travel into other planes of consciousness to learn from light beings as well as other souls. Now I teach others to do the same. As I co-write this book with Anna, I am excited to use my soul gifts.

As I move forward with my life work, I am excited to extend my hand and my heart to those who want to embrace that they too are incarnated souls. "Conscious Construction of the Soul" has been written at this time to help personalities begin to shift and bring forth the creative expression of their own soul, guides and teachers. I want to teach people they can also have direct connection to soul and things of spirit, including loved ones who have birthed into spirit. I want to teach people that when physical death occurs, consciousness continues. I know today as I write this book with Anna, what makes me different is that I am fully conscious. I am walking this earth walk guided by my soul and spiritual teachers.

The information contained in these pages is co-written by "Anna."

"Anna" has described themselves as a group of souls who no longer experience consciousness on earth. We use the name Anna because I, Katye, first experienced Anna as a part of myself, which is correct, for we are all connected. The core difference is I am still in the reincarnation cycle and I am experiencing consciousness on the earth planes of consciousness in a physical body. Anna experiences consciousness on the Astral and Causal planes of consciousness. Note to reader: All planes of consciousness exist within Creator God, also known as the universe.

Many people have asked me if I am channeling Anna. I have never used this term because Anna is a part of my consciousness. The information flows into me as a steady stream of higher light consciousness.

Together Anna and I take you on a journey. One which we hope will help others shift and bring into their consciousness that "humans" are incarnated souls living on the earth plane for the purpose of soul growth and expansion. In writing "Conscious Construction of the Soul" our desire is to bring into consciousness of the evolving human experience that life does not begin or end with the birth or death of the personality. In 2012, a shift occurred on the earth planes of consciousness. The mass populations on the planet earth did not consciously experience the shift. However, many incarnated beings did experience an awakening and a thirst for information which will help them evolve.

Conscious Construction of the Soul was written by me, asking Anna questions. The majority of the book was written while my, physical body was in a semi sleep state. This allowed for me to "travel" out of my physical body to other planes of consciousness. Anna encouraged me to use my gifts of clear sight and traveling into the astral, causal and Akashic planes of consciousness to bring forth descriptions as experienced by me. In the beginning of our work together, I usually had no conscious understanding of the experience until I was fully awake. As I began to relax into allowing Anna to speak through and with me, I began experiencing the teachings of Anna as they have been written in this book. We have tried to maintain the integrity of the transcripts as they were given to me.

Writing this book has allowed me to embrace more of my soul's gift. I am honored and humbled that my soul planned such a grand life for this incarnation. My personality, my soul and Anna are truly working in partnership to bring forth this work.

Blessings, Katye Anna

CHAPTER 1

THE BEGINNING
OF CONSCIOUSNESS
ON EARTH

Anna: We would like to begin by talking about Mother Earth. Mother Earth is a relatively young planet only being a few billion years old. It took the great Mother Earth billions of years as she went through her own evolutionary process. Mother Earth has her own consciousness, as does every inhabitant on her. Creator God sent forth sparks of itself into the universe. Each spark contained the creative intelligence of Creator God. Mother Earth, Father Sun and Mother Moon all worked in harmony as they each went through their own evolutionary processes. Today in the era of which we speak there is little understanding that Mother Earth itself is a living creation of God and is still on her own evolutionary process.

It was Mother Earth herself who invited other forms of consciousness to come and help her create. It took a few billion years or so before Mother Earth was inhabitable. During this time those of us who were created as smaller sparks of consciousness experienced consciousness as stars. We journeyed through time and space expanding, growing and evolving. Some sparks journeyed into the vast universe ready to create and experience consciousness in what would be known to you as other worlds.

As stars, we began to form clusters of consciousness and began to share our experiences with each other. We were of the light. Mother Earth continued to evolve, and many clusters of stars began to be drawn to her. It was Mother Earth herself who invited us to come and experience what she had created.

Being young forms of consciousness we wanted to experience more of our own creative energy. After all, this was our only direction from that which we came, go forth and experience consciousness. We welcomed the opportunity to join with Mother Earth to create a new consciousnesses, all contained within the universe of Creator God. We had evolved from individual sparks to clusters of star consciousness. We helped to create other galaxies as well as give birth to our own stars which we created through thought and sound.

Slowly we began focusing our consciousness on Mother Earth. Eventually we began to send sparks of ourselves into the depths of Mother Earth's ocean floors. Each star in the heavens has its own unique vibration. Understand, our original design still exists as the beautiful spark contained within the universal intelligence. We began to create through projecting our creative consciousness onto that which we wanted to create. The evolutionary process of Mother Earth slowly took shape and form. As evolving forms of consciousness, we had learned to allow our creative expression to find its own sacred rhythm.

Our star ancestors who had traveled and created forms of life in other galaxies taught us how to create in this new way. We began creating plant and mineral forms of life. Understand, this was all through sound and thought. It was with great excitement that we created new life within the depths of the ocean. Mother Earth continued to evolve. As our consciousness expanded within the depths of the sea, our ancestors, the plant life and mineral life, took shape and form. They were the first true inhabitants of the earth plane. Dolphins and whales took shape and form. These creations of consciousness were created through thought, light and sounds.

After much time we began to create on the surface of Mother Earth. Again, the form we used was very liquid, as was the structure of things. The evolutionary process on the earth plane was like none other. We slowly evolved. As Mother Earth took shape and form, we grew and expanded our consciousness along with her. Each infinite spark of the Creative Intelligence grew in consciousness and began bringing forth more of its individuality on the earth plane. Many of us experienced consciousness through plant and mineral life for thousands of earth years. Eventually we began to create mammal life and we grew in consciousness as well. As Mother Earth evolved we evolved.

Our evolutionary process began as a creative spark cast from Creator God. As we expanded our consciousness we found ourselves drawn to Mother Earth. Our desire to create continued to evolve. As with all growth and expansion, we learned to grow with the ebb and flow of that which we created.

Through our evolutionary process, the human form as you know it today has gone through many structural changes. Our physical forms were once more fluid. We created in unity through an expanded state of love. Slowly as more and more sparks were drawn to Mother Earth, our experiences expanded, as did our consciousness. As individual expressions of love we found the need to cycle off Mother Earth. We learned how to move our consciousness to what we now call the astral plane of existence. As we did this we began to understand that, even though we had cycled off Mother Earth, everything we had created remained on Mother Earth.

Creating, recreating and creating became the norm. We began to understand what was created on Mother Earth in the form of creative energy could not be destroyed. We learned that energy once created would exist forever in one form or the other. Our dance of creating began to spiral out of control. Before we knew it, many forms of consciousness began to abandon Mother Earth. They took no responsibility for that which they had created.

We gathered in the astral planes of consciousness. Those of us who were dedicated and loved Mother Earth agreed that we would finish that which we had begun eons ago. Meaning we would not leave Mother Earth nor abandon that which had been created. We knew, or at least we thought we understood what we had committed ourselves to. Of course, being young sparks of consciousness we had no idea what we were committing to. We didn't understand that our commitment to Mother Earth and that which had been created would lead us onto this evolutionary process.

It was during this time that what is known to us as our souls were created. As the star remained in the heavens, the soul would stay in the astral planes of consciousness. In this way we began to create, fully understanding that every incarnation we created would return to the astral plane as a stream of consciousness, one for which we were responsible.

Katye: Anna, as you spoke those last words, I began sobbing and I heard myself saying how much I longed to be pure light again. I found myself wanting to be connected to Creator God the way I was in the beginning. My cellular

19

memory still contains my original divine blueprint as I was cast from within Creator God. How did we evolve into souls who created what seems to be a world where love is not the guiding force? Hatred and greed among humankind seem to be the guiding force for many on this planet in the era of 2014. I understand that my soul is one of millions of souls who remain dedicated to seeing through that which we have created on Mother Earth. How will we ever return Mother Earth and all her inhabitants to a vibration of love?

I understand that what is known to me as Anna is a group of 1050 Souls who formed consciousness from star clusters eons ago evolved into what we call homo-sapiens. I am filled with hope because I know that a major shift in consciousness has occurred on Mother Earth and we are evolving into homospiritus. Meaning we are bringing more light into the physical form we currently use to navigate the earth planes of consciousness.

I also understand now why twenty-four years ago when I had my soul realignment, also known as a nervous breakdown, I would go out at night and cry asking the stars to take me home. I longed for the energy of the stars, which I now understand was my original design billions of years ago. Anna, am I truly billions of years old? Was I a star?

Anna: Yes, Katye, our origin can be traced back to the stars. It is also true we were created within the Universal Intelligence of what we refer to as Creator God billions of years ago. We remind you, when we use the term Creator God we do not refer to the Gods of religions. Remember, within Creator God there is no separation of time, distance, or lives lived. Because we are infinite sparks of Creator God we are always connected. What you experience as a longing for God is truly only experienced by the personality. Soul understands that there is no separation. We are all truly connected.

We might add here that the star that you asked to take you home those many years ago still exists.

We realize this discourse will open many doors for more discussions. It is important to understand how we have arrived at this place of consciousness. The focus of our work together is to bring forth a remembrance that we are souls who have chosen to experience life on Mother Earth through the reincarnation cycle. We offer our teachings to those who are ready to understand that they are multifaceted beings of love.

We would like to continue our next discourse with how souls currently create an incarnation on the earth planes of consciousness.

CHAPTER TWO

CREATION BEINGS ON
THE ASTRAL PLANES

Anna: The journey of soul returning to the earth plane of consciousness begins when the soul has decided it is time to create a new incarnation for soul growth and soul expansion. A soul is not limited to only creating on the earth planes of consciousness. In the astral planes of experience, soul is fully conscious of the truth that it is a spark of Creator God. As a spark of Creator God it was sent forth to expand the consciousness of the universal intelligence.

Souls understand that it is only on the earth plane of consciousness that one falls into a dream state of forgetting the truth of who it is, a spark of God, both creator and created. When a soul feels an inner knowing that it is ready to reincarnate, it begins the creative process of creating the desired incarnation. This process begins as all creation does, on the astral planes. Each soul has a council of wisdom, spirit guides and soul family who help them in this process. However it is up to each soul to create its own life plan. There are many tools available to the soul as it begins contemplating the many choices which will form the new incarnation. This includes a screening room where the soul can preview many different scenarios that may occur on the earth planes of consciousness.

Katye: Anna, are you telling me that on the astral plane a soul can have previews of what might occur during an incarnation?

Anna: Yes, this is correct. The soul views everything from a place of non- attachment. This, of course, is something which many personalities spend thousands of lifetimes learning on the earth planes of experience.

In helping you to understand the process a soul goes through during the pre-birthing plan, we will use the example of a soul we shall call Samuel. Samuel's soul has carefully reviewed its past incarnations. Understand, upon physical death consciousness continues. The soul will create a life based on what has returned to the astral planes of consciousness after each incarnation. In the case of Samuel's soul there have been several lives where the personalities of this soul have imprinted shame, guilt and rejection.

One past life experience was when Samuel's soul had created an incarnation as a girl. Her family had travelled by wagon train to have the dream of owning land in the new frontier of the western world. The family had created a nice life and the personality known as Carrie experienced life as peaceful at the young age of six. One day however this changed when the family's homestead was attacked by Indians. The young girl was taken and raised as an Indian.

Now understand here, after she got over the loss of her family she began to thrive as an Indian. She was happy and enjoyed her life living in nature and she thrived, even though she was rejected by many of the Indians as the white girl. She grew into a woman of strength and was chosen as the partner to one of the powerful young tribesman. She felt loved and had two children. After she had been with her native family for twelve years she was forced to return to life in a settlement. Her children were allowed to return with her, but her powerful young tribesman had been killed in the raid of the American soldiers. Understand here, the solders believed they were freeing the young woman from a life of tyranny.

At the age of eighteen the young woman now returned to the white man with her young children. Her mother and two brothers were still alive and welcomed Carrie back into their lives. However they rejected her children, and they rejected her wanting to be called by her Indian name. Others in the town rejected her and cast feelings of shame upon her for having had children by a heathen. As time went on she longed for her days with her Indian family. She was raped by several townsmen.

The people in the town were cruel and felt she was unclean by having been with her Indian lover, a man she had loved.

Slowly as time went on, her spirit was broken and she imprinted shame. She was torn between the love of her Indian family and what others were telling her about the heathens who took her and ruined her life. She imprinted shame, and her heart was broken as she mourned the loss of her Indian family. When she died at the young age of twenty-eight, she took back to soul many lessons of strength for she had thrived when many would not. However she also took back the imprinting of shame, rejection and guilt and her soul knew it would want to go back someday and heal these wounds.

After this lifetime the soul experienced two more lifetimes where shame, guilt and rejection continued. In one lifetime Samuel's soul was a man who rejected his family for being of Irish descent. He wanted to belong to those in a higher social class and so at the age of eighteen he told his newfound friends that his family had all died in a house fire. He changed his name and created a life built on lies and rejected his family. He was given many opportunities to reconnect with his family, but denied their existence. Although he achieved fame and success, he never was able to truly allow anyone to know him because of all his secrets. He died a wealthy man but a lonely man who had built his life on lies and rejection of those who loved him.

As we have said, consciousness continues after physical death. A soul is very aware of that which has been created by the personality during an incarnation.

As the soul reviews many of its personality's choices and lives it could clearly see a pattern of rejection, shame and guilt had manifested. Understanding this, the soul who would be born as Samuel was determined to create a life where it would release and heal the imprinting of shame, rejection and guilt.

You might ask why this is of any importance since the soul does not judge experiences as good or bad. This is true, however each soul fully understands how the energies of shame, guilt and rejection creates an environment on the earth plane which unleashes disease and destruction.

AIDS would be a disease which would have its roots in shame, guilt and rejection on the earth plane. In fact all auto immune diseases have their roots in shame, guilt and emotions of rejection and self-loathing. The body of the personality begins to turn on itself and create disease.

The soul, knowing that its life experiences contributed to the energy which grew into a disease called AIDS, now wanted to focus on creating a life where it would help to change the energy. The energy of AIDS is built on shame, guilt and rejection. Samuel wanted to change the energy into self-love, pride and dignity. This is why he chose to incarnate as a gay man in the era of 1950's.

 Having seen in the pre-life review, Samuel knew that AIDS would run rampant among gay men in the 70's and 80's. Samuel understood there would be the possibility that his personality could develop AIDS. He also understood there would be opportunities to use the chosen experiences to bring forth great healing for himself and many others.

The soul would download the code for AIDS, as well as the code for healing of AIDS into Samuel's DNA. The code for healing AIDS would be unleashed if the personality was successful in embracing a life of pride instead of shame.

After Samuel's soul chose its desired life experiences and the era, it now had to find other souls who would help create experiences where he would have the opportunity to heal rejection and shame.

Katye: Anna, are you saying that a soul willingly creates a life where it will experience rejection and shame? Why would a soul choose to create a life where they know the personality is going to suffer?

Anna: Katye, souls do not create lives in which the personality will suffer. Suffering is manifested on the earth plane of experience. As a part of the pre-birthing plan, a soul can choose what experiences it thinks will help to create an environment for soul growth and expansion. It is for this reason that Samuel chose to create a life where his personality would have the opportunity to transcend the experiences of rejection and shame.

The next step in the creative process of the construction of the soul is selecting other souls it will incarnate with.

Katye: You are saying that we choose the other souls who will be a part of our chosen life experiences?

Anna: Yes, souls have soul families. These soul families consist of 1050 different souls.

Katye: Wow! So you are saying we reincarnate with the same group of souls every lifetime?

Anna: Yes, this is what we are saying. The roles and life lessons will be different, depending on the desired lessons and chosen experiences for soul growth and expansion. Now that Samuel has chosen his desired goals and era, his soul begins the creative process of choosing other souls who will help him by creating the desired experiences.

Again, souls go through many degrees of understanding what may or may not occur during the incarnation, depending on the experiences and imprinting of the personality. Samuel chose to be born to a mother and father who wanted to experience acceptance as a goal. As a part of the soul contract, his chosen father agreed that he would create experiences where he would teach his son about acceptance through experiences of rejection.

The soul who would be known as Samuel's father agreed to do this for Samuel out of love. The soul understood that he would have to reject his son as part of the experiences that they both desired unless he had himself learned acceptance. Understand that Samuel's chosen father wanted to create a life where he would learn acceptance of self and others. To do this, he agreed to participate in Samuel's desired experiences of being rejected and shamed. By agreeing to be a father who would reject his gay son, both souls knew this would create an environment where both souls could choose to grow in love. Of course seeing the many possibilities which could happen during the incarnation, the souls knew they would have to plan wisely.

The soul who agreed to be Samuel's mother was also one of the souls who had rejected Samuel's personality known as Carrie in the lifetime during the 1800's. This soul wanted to help Samuel heal these wounds that it had helped to create.

Katye: Let me be clear here, Anna. You are saying that Samuel's soul chose to create a life with another soul it knew had caused him emotional harm in another life? Why would he want to do this, why not choose a soul who had been loving and kind during a past incarnation?

Anna: Katye, please understand, souls do not judge other souls and the experiences as good or bad. Souls understand that each soul creates lives for soul growth and soul expansion. The earth plane is a place where there is duality. Personalities learn from both the light and the shadow elements of experiences. Samuel chose the soul who would be his mother knowing their desired goals could serve each other's life plan. In this lifetime the soul chosen as Samuel's mother wanted to create a life where it would have the opportunity to change the energy of rejection from the past incarnation into one of love and acceptance. This soul had had many lives where it had the opportunity to speak in love and did not, usually because of fear of being judged and rejected by others. In the created process of the pre-birthing plan, Samuel's soul agreed that this would give them both an opportunity for soul growth and soul expansion.

His mother agreed to create experiences where she would help Samuel experience self-worth. Part of their soul contract was that Samuel's mother would help Samuel love and embrace himself as a gay man. Both souls clearly understood there was always the possibility that Samuel's mother's personality would not find the courage and the strength to stand up for her son. The soul who agreed to be Samuel's father also agreed to be the one who would continually create experiences where his wife would have the opportunity to stand up for her son. All souls involved clearly understood that they were agreeing to these chosen roles from a place of love. Samuel's father's soul reminded both Samuel and his chosen wife that while on the earth plane both would forget that he was doing this from a place of love.

Katye: Why do personalities have to forget that experiences were chosen for soul growth and soul expansion?

Anna: The earth plane of experience is one of duality. Souls understand this before incarnating. Souls also understand that, because the earth plane of existence is such a dense field of energy, try as they may, the incarnating personality does not retain the memories of being a soul. Nor do they remember the pre-birthing plan and soul agreements. We will say that, as the consciousness of personalities continues to evolve, a remembrance of being an incarnated soul is beginning to occur on the earth plane. This is one reason we are writing this book with you: to help personalities remember the truth of their creation.

The souls journeying with Samuel all understood that forgetting the pre-birthing plan and soul contract would not be a conscious process. All souls are also aware of the ongoing soul essence contact they would have during sleep time. This soul essence contact helps to keep the personality on track with the soul's plans.

As part of the pre-birthing plan and soul contract, the soul who would be Samuel's father agreed to the role of the one who would reject his son. This soul chose to be a minister of a religion that totally would denounce gays as sinners. This soul did this because it wanted the opportunity to grow into acceptance of that which he denied and rejected as evil. By agreeing to be a personality who would reject his son, the life plan for Samuel could be played out as well as his own.

Samuel had clear goals of embracing himself as a gay man who would not develop AIDS. The mother had the clear goal of embracing her son and supporting him during the difficult years of being a young boy and knowing he's different from his friends. This soul would also have the opportunity to stand up to Samuel's father, her husband, in support of their son. The soul chosen as the father understood that it would be given the opportunity to love and embrace his son in the later years of life. It clearly understood that he would be seen as the one who was a minister and preached love but rejected his own son.

Knowing the pre-birthing plans and the soul contracts, the soul goes to work to create a support system for the incarnation it is creating. They do this by choosing spirit guides and helpers, as well as choosing other souls who would support the desired experiences.

In the case of Samuel, his soul chose Archangel Michael and Archangel Zophkiel as two guardians who would travel to the earth plane and be available to help Samuel during his life experiences.

Katye: Most people have no concept that they are a soul. Nor do they know they have spirit guides who can help them.

Anna: Yes, we are aware that spirit guides and matters of the soul have been lost for thousands of years on the earth plane. However there is desire by many to embrace the path of love. We believe many are ready to embrace the truth that they are incarnated souls.

Samuel's soul understood that Samuel would experience times of great fear during his lifetime. Archangel Michael was chosen as a guide to help Samuel see through the fear and embrace his power. This is why Archangel Zophkiel was chosen. Archangel Zophkiel would help Samuel bring forth his power.

Samuel continued the pre-birthing process by choosing when he would be born. He also chose attributes such as body type, ethnic background, place and time of birth and other life experiences for soul growth and expansion.

Samuel spoke to the council of wisdom and clearly understood the challenges he would face as a gay man. He understood being born in the era of 1953, to a minister living in the Bible Belt in the state of Texas would be difficult. He also understood that his goal of being a gay man and letting others know would bring many different experiences. These experiences could have him do the very opposite of his goal which would be to imprint more shame and guilt. Samuel's soul believed it had chosen wisely. His choices of family and place of birth would help him create an environment where his personality would have the strength and courage to bring forth the creative expression of his soul.

Before beginning his journey, there was only one thing left to do on the astral plane. Samuel had to finalize the soul contracts with the other souls who would be journeying with him during this incarnation.

Many other souls would agree to be a part of Samuel's journey. A few of these souls would have great influence over Samuel's life. One soul agreed to be a teacher who Samuel would meet in the eighth grade. This soul agreed to be a gay teacher because he wanted to help Samuel and other souls be empowered. Samuel also chose a soul who would be his sister. This soul agreed to be daddy's little girl knowing that at some point in her life she would have to choose to reject Samuel or stand up to her father who would adore her. In previous lives this soul stood by and allowed others to be persecuted for crimes they had not done. Her goal in this incarnation would be to stand up to bullies and to support her brother. However both Samuel's soul and the soul who would be his sister understood that the personality might choose a very different path. Samuel also chose other souls who would be lovers as well as a soul who would play the role of a female wanting to be Samuel's girlfriend. This soul had experienced rejection in many past lives. In the life she agreed to play the role of a young woman who would fall in love with Samuel. Although Samuel would love her it would never be more than as a dear friend.

As Samuel began to bring together the details of his incarnation, there would be one more very important step before he incarnated as Samuel. It was now time for all souls who would have soul contracts with Samuel to seal the contracts.

CHAPTER THREE

THE HALL OF RECORDS AND SOUL CONTRACTS

November 23rd 2013

Katye: It is 4:23AM. I have been awake for some time but stayed in bed. I have many questions and look forward to my time together with Anna. I have found that asking questions is our format for learning. I ask and Anna teaches. When I begin to write, I am aware that Anna and other teachers from the higher astral planes and other planes of consciousness begin to make their way known to me. I have consciously agreed to bring forth the teachings of Anna. I have a few questions about soul contracts. As I am writing,

I remember being shown what a soul contract "looks" like in the astral plane.

Please keep in mind that my words will never express what I was shown, however I feel it's important to try.

Katye: This morning I was taken to the Hall of Records.

When I think of the soul records, I think of life events being stored in the hall of records. I've had access to these records for some time. My guide into the records has been Jasper. Jasper and many guides like him are souls who have chosen to continue expanding consciousness on this plane of existence, which is called the Akashic plane.

Jasper took me to the Akashic plane of consciousness. Until now I understood this plane of consciousness to be where the experiences and knowledge of the universe are recorded. I always thought of the Akashic records as containing knowledge of past events. Jasper assured me that this is correct; however he wanted to show me another "place" within this plane of consciousness.

This morning I was given entrance to a part of the soul records where I have never been; at least I had no conscious awareness of this place. Jasper led me through what seemed to be halls and halls of records until we came to a beautiful vaulted area. I could see colors of golden light glowing from within the chamber. As the door to the chamber opened up I was in awe of what I was seeing. There were souls everywhere. They were writing on what appeared to be some kind of paper. (This paper was not physical.) There were also Angelics in the chamber as well as many other beings of light in this hall of records. It was a place of tranquility and much like our libraries are on the physical plane. It was a very peaceful place.

Jasper explained to me that this is the place souls come to finalize their soul contracts. It is here where souls gather to bring into context the life plan they have created for their chosen incarnation. It is also a realm of consciousness where souls are asked one more time if the soul plan is fully understood.

Anna: Keep in mind that each soul incarnates for its own purpose. Bringing together the desires and creations of soul is no minor undertaking, as one would imagine. This is why soul contracts are of major importance in the "Conscious Construction of the Soul". It is here in this chamber of records that Souls make a sacred and binding covenant with each other.

Katye: I remember being in awe as I watched souls who agreed to participate in the journey of another soul.

Anna: Souls involved in the contracts are very aware that, upon entrance into the physical plane, the personality may create a life that has little to do with the chosen soul plans. This gives whole new meaning to our soul agreements. Souls include in the agreements that each soul is connected and is dependent on one another to bring forth, into the physical plane, the life plan of the other souls they have soul contracts with.

Katye: Anna explained to me that, each soul creates its own life plan and incarnates for its own purposes. They do so understanding that there is no "I" on any plane of existence other than the earth plane. We are each connected, a part of the whole, a part of the sum of itself.

Anna: Do you understand this? It's true that each soul's life plan is created with experiences the soul desires to create on the physical plane. Souls are dependent on the soul agreements that each soul will be what they have been asked to be. This ensures the experiences of both souls are fulfilled. This means of course that each soul life plan is connected. There is no separation, no "I". There is only oneness and unity.

Do you understand what we are teaching you here?

Katye: I do have questions, and I must admit my head is spinning. I understand that each soul's life plan is created for its own purpose. I don't understand how souls are dependent on a soul agreement that each soul will be what is needed to ensure that the creation of the other is fulfilled.

Anna: Souls understand what is quickly forgotten on the earth plane. We are each connected, a part of the whole, a part of the sum of itself. Therefore for each soul's life plan to succeed there must be a spirit of co-operation and oneness. As our friend Jasper has shown you, soul agreements and contracts are entered into with holy alliance and with humble devotion. It would do well for those of you in physical embodiments to remember this.

One will know that the soul contract is being fulfilled when one begins to see the ebb and flow to life's circumstances. If one is in a holy alliance, one will understand that life events and situations are simply an outward manifestation of the human experience. Keep in mind here that the created personality has free will. The contracts of souls include helping each other in the physical remember the truth behind their creation, which is soul growth and expansion.

In the hall of records, the souls who are incarnating gather together to seal together their chosen journeys. Souls understand that that which has been created in higher planes of consciousness must now be created in the denseness of the physical plane of consciousness. Each indwelling soul watches as the seal is placed upon the holy plan.

When the chosen time arrives, the soul begins the descent into the physical plane, leaving behind soul family and those who remain in other planes of consciousness within Creator God. Remember, all souls choose to embark on this journey knowing that it is both creator and creation. Having no illusion of time or separation, the soul sets forth on its journey knowing it does so with the full resource of the entire universe.

Katye: Anna, why does the Soul leave a place where there is only love for a place, the earth plane, where there is separation? Why would one ever leave to experience the challenges of the physical plane?

Anna: The soul understands what you have not yet integrated: that one never leaves love. Love is always and forever. Love simply changes form, be it on the higher planes of consciousness or the earth planes.

As our friend Jasper has showed you, all soul agreements and contracts are entered into with holy alliance and with humble devotion.

Katye, do you understand what we are conveying here? We feel this is a very important teaching of light for students of earth to remember. What would life be like if you understood that behind every human experience there is a holy soul alliance? Yes, it is true many personalities stray far from the chosen life plan of the soul. If those on earth began to learn from this teaching of light that everyone is connected, a part of the whole, the earth plane could begin to heal.

Katye: I am being shown Samuel and the many souls who will be journeying with him. It's very beautiful and I have a feeling of wonderment as I embrace the truth that, as an incarnated being, I too have gathered with those in my life to form sacred contracts. It's a very humbling experience to know this.

I continue to watch as Samuel and those who will be a part of his earth journey are asked one last time by the great council of wisdom if they want to finalize their soul agreements. The soul who is to be Samuel's father looks at Samuel and reminds him again that it is agreeing to help him learn self love and empowerment. As a part of the soul agreement, it is clear that many years could be experienced as a time filled with very painful experiences. The two souls look at each other and my heart is overflowing with love for these souls as they both fully understand the gift of love they are giving each other.

They have both chosen some very hard lessons and understand that their personalities may never reach the place of experiencing the love these two Souls share for each other.

I also watch as several souls gather around Samuel and begin finalizing their journey together. I understand that these souls have agreed to be Samuel's lovers and teachers and what we call soul companions. It is through watching these souls that I understand that we truly have many soul agreements with those we have lover relationships with.

I watch as these souls begin to finalize the plans for soul growth and expansion. I am shown several soul agreements Samuel is making with souls who will be major participants in Samuel's journey.

Soul One agrees to be Samuel's teenage lover who will bring the realization to Samuel that he gay. This soul agrees to bring forth a multitude of lessons including shame, joy, love, rejection and acceptance. This soul has chosen as its life lesson to be a gay man who rejects his homosexuality and also rejects Samuel. The relationship between Samuel and Soul One will be a very difficult one for both souls. Samuel and Soul One are, once again, asked if they fully understand that, for the personality, their relationship will be experienced as a very difficult experience. I watch as Samuel and Soul One exchange a few moments of connection before they both agree to the very difficult soul lessons contained in their soul contacts. They both understand that they will each be what the other needs them to be to ensure that the life plan of each soul will be successful.

Soul Two agrees to be Samuel's lover who teaches Samuel about self-love. Samuel and Soul Two agree to meet around the sixteenth to seventeenth year of life. Soul Two life's plan is to have fun in this lifetime. Soul Two wants to have life experiences in which it will learn about the importance of healthy boundaries. To learn about boundaries, his life plan includes having parents who go to Samuel's father's church. Soul Two agreed to lessons which will impose strict rules within the family about right and wrong. Soul Two's parents have also agreed to believe in a God who rejects homosexuals. All souls know Creator God rejects no one. Soul Two's chosen parents both want to learn about acceptance and unconditional love. As a part of the soul agreement, Soul Two has agreed to be a homosexual young male who challenges the authority of those around him. Soul Two will teach Samuel's personality courage and self-love.

Soul Three agrees to be a female Samuel uses to hide the truth that he is a gay young man. Soul Three wants to learn about forgiveness. Soul Three agrees to be Samuel's girlfriend in high school. Part of the soul plan includes Samuel struggling with being gay and Soul Three struggles with allowing others to use her. Soul Three's life plans include learning about self-love as well as learning about empowerment and self-worth. Samuel's soul plan also includes learning about self-love. Having the goal of learning about self-worth is one reason they have chosen to journey together. Samuel's soul agrees to teach Soul Three about self-love as he uses her to hide from himself and others that he is gay. Both Souls understand their personalities will have many opportunities for growth in their soul lessons. Both Souls understand that their personalities might imprint resentment. Soul Three will also imprint being a victim, but the clear goal of the Soul Three is to embrace self-love and not give her power away to anyone. Soul Three understands she will have the opportunity to learn forgiveness when the personality discovers Samuel being sexual with another boy.

I watch as Samuel continues to make soul agreements with many other souls. Some will reject Samuel for being gay, others will encourage him to shine. The soul which will be his sister has a special soul agreement with Samuel. Their relationship will have many twists and turns, especially during childhood. Samuel's sister has chosen the goal of service. This soul has chosen to be a part of Samuel's family because it has a very strong archetypal influence of the prostitute and pleaser. Having the goal of service, it is clear to me she will face many challenges of not falling into the shadow energy of submission. The contract with her brother is clear. This soul will have many opportunities to stand up for her brother Samuel. This will allow this soul to stand in her truth and not please her very strict father to dictate how she should feel. This soul is very aware that it has had many past incarnations where the strong influences of pleaser and prostitute energy influenced her in negative ways.

Soul Four will be the soul Samuel meets in his late teens, who will be one of Samuel's committed relationships. Both souls fall in love under the veil of secrecy and being kicked out of the service if anyone were to discover their secret. Soul Four will die of AIDS. Samuel will still be enlisted and on active duty in the service. This of course will give both souls major life lessons. Their soul agreement is clearly one that is meant to offer both souls major growth opportunities. Soul Four will also be downloaded with the AIDS virus and, in fact, will turn on the code for the disease and eventually die of AIDS. Soul Four will have a great sense of peace about his journey with AIDS and his agreement to die in his mid thirties. The timeline will have many variables. Both souls clearly understand that the relationship will be one where Samuel will experience much joy and yes much grief. This will all occur as Samuel continues to be in the military hiding the fact that he is a gay man.

Soul Five will be a man with whom Samuel has another partner agreement and will be Samuel's life partner until they transition. Soul Five will be married and have four children when Samuel and Soul Five meet sometime during Samuel's forties. They will meet after Samuel is out of the service and free to let others know he is gay. Together these souls will find their way as men who are gay and proud. Their soul agreement will offer both the opportunity to help other gay men and women embrace themselves. Both Samuel and Soul Five will spend their lives fighting for equal rights for gays. They have a strong soul agreement to bring forth confidence and pride in each other and the many lives they will touch. In the year of 2013 Samuel and Soul Five marry in the state of California where they will live out their lives.

Anna: Please remember, these soul agreements are sacred and binding. Souls understand that the personality may stray from the chosen life plan of the soul. Samuel will choose several different souls who could be his life partner and help Samuel with his personal goals of being an activist for gay rights. This is a major part of Samuel's life plan. His soul has looked at many variables that will ensure his plan to be an activist for gay rights. His soul has chosen many different plans to ensure his personality will find its way to this chosen soul goal.

Katye: Wow! I can clearly see how our souls create our lives through life lessons. Anna, I'm amazed as I watch these souls as they agree to the life lessons and soul contracts.

They all seem excited and have such enthusiasm for what they are creating. The souls are pleased with their chosen life lessons. They have created many scenarios which will give the opportunity for soul growth and expansion.

Katye: Anna, my attention is being drawn to the big viewing screen. In front of my eyes I watch what appears to be tens of thousands of souls viewing the screen. My heart is overcome with grief as I watch the many thousands of souls who agree to teach about compassion through AIDS. My heart is heavy as I watch the screen knowing how many will die of AIDS and how many more will experience rejection and shame through the experience of AIDS. Tears flow as I begin to understand the souls who choose to teach humanity through mass experiences such as AIDS.

Anna, can you help me understand the bigger lesson here?

Anna: Yes, Katye, we feel your grief as you begin to understand the impact of soul lessons through mass teachings such as AIDS. The souls you see watching the viewing screen are doing so before they agree to the soul contract. For many who are agreeing to be part of the AIDS experience they do so for many reasons. The disease of AIDS is rooted in the energy of fear, shame, guilt and rejection. All souls who agree to participate in the mass lesson of AIDS are doing so to help those on the earth plane learn about love and compassion. They also want to confront fear, hatred and rejection of those who are gay.

Millions of personalities' lives with be impacted by AIDS. The opportunity for soul growth and expansion are endless. Every effort has been made to help souls understand the soul lessons and the impact on humanity.

The souls who choose to participate in AIDS do so wanting to change the energy which created AIDS from past incarnations.

Katye: I'm just amazed as I begin to understand the process souls go through before incarnating.

Anna: In the case of Samuel, the goal of his soul is not to open the code for AIDS. His life will be greatly affected by the deaths of many friends. There will be fear surrounding AIDS.

Katye: The opportunities for soul growth are amazing. My own life was greatly influenced by men and women with AIDS. It was working at the York House Hospice for AIDS that I made the decision to dedicate my life to helping people live conscious lives so they could die consciously. I can also see how we have many soul mates chosen by our souls as a part of our life plan and soul contract. I know I had soul contracts from those men and women I met at the hospice.

Anna: Yes, each soul chooses many souls to journey with them as what you call a soul mate. The term soul mate has been reduced to love relationships for the personality. Souls understand that every relationship is a sacred relationship. Souls prefer the term soul partnership. We would offer here a soul understanding that every relationship, big or small, is a sacred and holy alliance between souls.

Older souls understand that personalities try to define relationships. Souls also understand that sacred and holy alliances between souls can never truly be defined. It would serve personalities to stop labeling relationships. Understand that those who are with you on your journey have a sacred and binding soul agreement to help one another bring forth lessons for soul growth and expansion. The value of soul lessons cannot be measured in the length of time or even the nature of the relationship.

Pillar of light we offer you now: begin to see every personality you meet as an incarnated soul with whom you have a sacred partnership. This soul partnership is not measured in time spent together, for the briefest life lesson offers opportunity for soul growth and expansion. Think about your life and the personalities who were in your life for a very brief time. Were not these experiences of great value?

Katye: Yes, Anna. At the age of 62, I understand how many of the twists and turns of my life were orchestrated by the grand design of my soul's life plan. Anna, as I stand in this hall of records, the love that these souls have for one another is all consuming. Tears flow from my eyes as I see the endless parade of souls preparing to leave this place of love to incarnate on the earth plane of consciousness.

I am aware now that the many souls surrounding Samuel are finalizing their soul contracts. The soul who will be Samuel's father is reaching out to Samuel one last time. He reminds him that their personalities will forget that the life experiences and the many twists and turns of their lives together were designed by their souls for soul growth and expansion. I can hear this soul saying to Samuel that it will do its best to bring forth the desired experiences.

I continue to watch the soul who has been chosen for Samuel's father. He is surrounded by other souls who seem to be offering encouragement. I am beginning to understand how souls who choose to participate in life lessons which could unleash hardship and pain during the incarnation do so yes, for their own soul growth and expansion, but also because love for one another soul is truly unconditional.

I am now thinking of those who have taught me some of my major life lessons. Anna, I would like to discuss in a later discourse how we can know when an experience is a chosen soul lesson, or is result of the personality's integration of life experiences?

Anna: We will briefly answer this question now. Souls understand the personality may have difficulty with the life plans and goals set forth in the soul contracts and agreements. It is for these reasons souls carefully choose other souls who will help the personality with many of the life events. Also remember, during the time when the physical body sleeps, the personality will travel to the astral plane. The personality will receive help and guidance from other souls and spirit teachers. If the personality cannot bring forth the desired growth and life lessons, the soul can always give the personality what is known as a soul realignment. Katye, you have referred to soul realignments as a "soul boot".

This simply means the soul will bring forth a challenge for the personality which will help the personality begin to rethink many of their life choices. This is often brought forth by an illness or, as in your case, Katye, a nervous breakdown. If doctors and the religious community were schooled in matters of the soul, they would understand that this is an indication that the personality needs to reevaluate its life choices and current path. We will discuss soul realignment in the chapter on soul energy healing.

Katye: Does every personality get a soul realignment?

Anna: With the help of the council of wisdom, a soul will decide if the personality has the strength and the endurance to receive a soul realignment. Because the personality has chosen to differ so far from the goals and plans of the soul, the soul may or may not choose to do a soul realignment. The soul always has the options to continue on the path set forth by the personality and use the life lessons as means of soul growth and expansion. Remember, Katye, the earth plane of consciousness is one of free will. Spirit guides and souls can encourage and direct the personality in dreamtime and through intuition. It is always the choice of the personality to ground these visions into its life.

After a soul realignment is given the personality will experience a time of great challenges. When this occurs the soul and spirit guides will begin to offer the personality life choices. These choices will help the personality shift from the current path to one which is in alignment with the soul's chosen life plan and goals.

Souls understand that even though a soul agreement is sacred and binding, it is always the choices of the personality which will determine the successful completion of the soul's life plan.

Souls understand that which has been created in higher planes of consciousness with holy alliance and humble devotion must now be created in the denseness of the physical plane of consciousness.

It is true many personalities may stray far from the chosen life plan of the Soul. If those on earth begin to learn from this teaching of light that everyone is connected, a part of the whole, a part of the sum of itself, the earth plane could begin to heal the energy of earth and all of her inhabitants consciously.

Again we remind you, soul agreements include sacred teachings of light. Each soul is connected and is dependent on each other to bring forth into the physical plane the life plans of the other souls they have soul contracts with.

Katye: I think this is indeed a very important understanding of soul contracts and agreements that has gotten lost here on the earth plane of consciousness. Most people see themselves as separated, not connected, but what you are clearly saying is that, for my soul to have its life plan succeed I must help to bring forth the life plans of the other souls I have a sacred partnership with.

Anna: We realize you have many more questions. If one is bringing forth the creative expression of the soul the personality will have a sense of knowing and even peace that all is well, no matter what the experience is. Personalities can learn the lessons of soul the easy or the hard way.

We now return your focus back to Samuel and the Hall of records.

Katye: I once again put my attention on Samuel and the many souls who will travel with him. In this chamber of soul contracts, I feel very emotional as I watch Samuel and the many souls who have agreed to participate with Samuel during this incarnation. I also see groups of Souls who have agreed to be souls who may never meet Samuel in the physical, but their personality's lives will be affected by Samuel.

I see incarnated souls who live in countries where Samuel would participate in service during his time in the military. I see souls whose lives will be affected by Samuel's activism for gay rights. I see souls who agree to have a brief defining moment during Samuel's life. These souls touch the lives of one another be it as a church member, a student in the schools, a military person, to the soul who simply passes Samuel by one day and a brief knowing is experienced by both.

I watch as Samuel's soul stands before the council of wisdom surrounded by the many souls and light beings which would participate in Samuel's incarnation. It is with great excitement that Samuel's soul signs the beautiful, sacred and binding soul agreement, which will be stored in the hall of records. As Samuel signs the soul agreement, there is silence. Each soul whose life will be affected by this soul agreement fully embraces the magnitude of what they have all agreed to. It is here that the agreement "to be that which you need me to be" is fully understood.

Slowly the souls begin to leave this chamber of records. They do so knowing that when the time is right they will meet on the earth plane of consciousness to bring forth what has been set forth and agreed upon in the astral plane of creation.

I watch as the souls who agreed to major roles in Samuel's incarnation connect one last time, and I hear the soul who has chosen to be Samuel's father tell Samuel, "Remember, I have agreed to be that which you need me to be, as you have agreed to be what I need you to be. Doing so will ensure that both of our life plans will be fulfilled. We do so from this place of love; may we seek to bring this forth on the earth plane someday."

CHAPTER FOUR

THE EARTH
JOURNEY BEGINS

Katye: I am still amazed at the process our souls go through to create a pre- birthing plan and soul contracts. Anna, how does a soul know when it's time to reincarnate?

Anna: Yes Katye, you are correct. Much thought, detail and collaboration goes into creating an incarnation. Souls use what is known as a creative process to create an incarnation. Once the soul contracts are agreed upon and signed, souls slowly return to the astral plane, where they continue evolving and growing. As is the case for all souls, Samuel will know when the time is right for him to begin the journey of descending into the earth planes of consciousness.

Samuel's soul has observed as his chosen parents have lived their lives on the earth plane. He clearly understands the personalities who are to be his parents have forgotten that they are incarnated souls. The personality which is to be his mother has grown into a woman who has no clear voice of her own. She is meek and obedient to the demands of her husband. Her name is Elizabeth. She is twenty-six years old and is a dutiful preacher's wife. The personality which is to be Samuel's father is a Bible thumping preacher saving souls. His voice is the only voice which is heard in the family. His name is William and his age is twenty-nine. Samuel will be their firstborn child.

As the time grows near for Samuel's earth journey to begin, Samuel's soul has one last life preview with all the many souls who have chosen to journey with him. The Souls who are to be his parents as well as Samuels soul are aware that the emotional climate in which Samuel will be born will be one which will create the environment where being a gay man born in the year 1953 will be challenging at best.

Samuel's soul essence hovers in the energy field of Elizabeth in the months before she becomes pregnant. Energetically this is the souls' way of supporting its mother to be. Slowly Samuel's soul begins to feel the pull of energy letting it know that Samuel's chosen mother has conceived. His soul begins to connect energetically with the fetus as well as Elizabeth. This is a beautiful time for

Elizabeth and the child which she holds within. Elizabeth knows she will do whatever she has to do to cover her child. She feels a deep emotional bond with her unborn child. Samuel's soul hovers around the energy field of Elizabeth. This is also a time of expectation for Samuel's soul. This growing fetus will be the vehicle for the creative expression of the soul. Samuel's soul, as many souls are, is ready to move ahead with its life plans. Having no need to experience childbirth Samuel's soul will fully enter the physical form of the body shortly after birth. This body will be the vehicle for his soul during this incarnation. As preplanned the baby is a healthy one.

Katye: Do some souls choose to unite with the fetus before childbirth? You have said that this is a choice of the soul.

Anna: Yes Katye, this is correct. According to each soul's life plan, the birth itself can be a major part of the chosen life experience. It is for this reason that each soul chooses when to enter into the physical form of the developing baby. Remember although the physical form is developing, it will be the home, as in Samuel's case, of a very old soul. All souls begin to weave the energetic structure of the soul during the last few months of physical growth.

Let us make clear here that, as the fetus is developing, the soul who has chosen to unite with the living life form is very involved and connected to the fetus and the mother, as the fetus goes through the developmental stages of physical growth. Samuel and all souls take a watchful approach as the fetus begins to develop. Just as the mother and father connect with the developing child during this process, Samuel also begins to connect with this life form, knowing that this will be his vehicle in which his soul will experience its chosen incarnation.

Although Samuel being an old soul has no need to experience childbirth, Samuel is involved with the growing fetus just as the physical parents are. It is with great excitement that Samuel connected with the fetus during this time of physical development.

Just as many parents and those connected to the baby, souls on the astral plane are excited to hear that Samuel's physical form is developing. It is during this time of physical development that Samuel and the other souls watch from the astral plane of creation as the fetus grows into the form which will be the vehicle used to bring forth the divine plan of the soul.

There is a time, especially a few weeks before birth, in which Samuel begins to feel the pull toward the developing baby. This begins the descent of spirit through the tunnel of light into the physical form. The bonding of soul to its chosen body begins to take shape and form as the soul begins to hover around the mother and growing life form during the last developmental stages of physical growth. When physical labor begins, the chosen spirit guides join the guides of those assisting during labor, as well as the guides of the parents.

As Samuel feels the vibrational pull telling his soul it is time, Samuel's soul begins to project its energy toward being born. Samuel fully understands the denseness of earth may make him forget that he is an incarnated soul. All souls know that, upon entering the earth planes of consciousness, there is a forgetting of the astral plane and the world of spirit.

On the earth plane of consciousness, Elizabeth has enjoyed her pregnancy. Her connection with her unborn child is one of love and concern as she begins the process of labor. William is away saving souls as she begins labor and her parents drive her to the hospital. As she labors alone in the sterile room the pain of childbirth is overwhelming. Unknown to Elizabeth, her spirit guides surround her doing what they can to comfort her, however she has long ago forgotten these helpers and has no idea of their support and guidance.

The labor is long and painful. Elizabeth grows weary and just when she thinks she can labor no more, her beautiful son is born. As the baby takes its first breath, Samuel's soul projects a spark of its soul essence containing the codes of light and divine blueprint which contain the chosen goals and path for its incarnation into the baby. As the umbilical cord is severed, the light body of soul gently surrounds the body.

With each breath the baby takes, it begins uniting with its soul. The heart, which once beat through the physical connection to the mother, now beats on its own. Although the umbilical cord has been severed, the cord of light connecting it to its soul is intact, establishing an eternal connection with one's soul and Creator God.

As was the experience in the year 1953, mother and child are temporarily separated as the nurses and doctor tend to their individual needs. It would do well for those in attendance when a baby is born to understand that which has taken place. A soul has set forth on a journey of life on the earth planes of consciousness. This beautiful creation is an incarnated soul and has many needs both physical and spiritual, however few souls are welcomed in those manner. If any acknowledgement is made spiritually, it's according to religious beliefs of those around the child.

It would do well for those around the incarnated soul to take a few moments and simply behold the wonder of that which has been created in love by a soul. A spark of Creator God has breathed life into this form of spirit and matter.

A simple blessing: Behold no greater gift than this has been given. What we speak here is the gift of life.

Anna: From the soul plane of creation, Samuel begins the final stages of soul development for the physical form as it begins to weave its unique soul essence and divine spark into the form of the laboring child. Communion with the soul has been ongoing during the development of fetus to a physical form which will house the spark of spirit, thus creating a spiritual being, one which is comprised of both physical and spiritual qualities.

The final stages of the merging the physical body being infused with the spark of spirit begins the journey of the soul on the earth plane of consciousness.

The physical form, which the parents will call Samuel, is contained by a field of pulsating magnetic field of energy. This form of light surrounding the physical body occurs upon birth. Until this time, the fetus depends upon the embryo sack in the mother's womb. At the severing of the cord, the soul sends forth the living spark of soul essence into the body of the newborn, and with it its energy bodies of light begin to take shape and form. With each physical breath, the light bodies and the physical form begin to give birth to the spiritual manifestation of the soul.

The soul has created a physical life form in which it will navigate the physical plane of reality. Just as the team of doctors and nurses, working to ensure that mother and child are taken care of during and after labor, there is a team of light beings helping to ground into the physical the spiritual form known as the light body, with the physical form of the child. Once the union of physical and spirit have merged the birthing process is complete. Life of the spiritual being begins with the severing of the cord.

Once dependent on the mother for each breath, the child now begins to breathe on its own and with each breath, grounds into the physical the essence of the soul which will experience life. This union and merging of soul essence and physical is a union of love both dependent on the other, for the soul has no life without the physical form and the physical form has no life without the soul.

Katye: Anna, what you are describing here is amazing. I have often wondered how the soul and the physical merge.

Anna: This is another pillar of "Conscious Construction of the Soul". The physical body is the vehicle for the soul. The physical body has no "life" without the soul. The soul has no physical life without the vehicle of the physical body. They are dependent upon each other, for a soul without a body has no human existence, and the body without a soul has no reason to exist. Do you understand what we are saying here?

Let us repeat this again. The physical body is the vehicle for the soul. The physical body has no "life" without the soul. The soul has no physical life without the vehicle of the physical body. They are dependent upon each other, for a soul without a body has no human existence and the body without a soul has no reason to exist, nor can it exist. It is the soul which gives life to the physical. It is truly this simple.

The sole purpose for the body is to provide a container/ vehicle for the soul. We realize that this statement can be off putting for most of humanity, because they have forgotten the truth of their creation. It would do well for mankind to remember the truth and validity of these words. The information in "Conscious Construction of the Soul" is to bring into remembrance the pillars of light which form the construction of the soul. The soul by itself is a creative spark of God. It is a multifaceted spiritual being, and is constantly creating on many planes of existence simultaneously. The soul does not need a physical body to create on any plane of creation other than the earth plane of consciousness.

Katye, we would like you to return your focus of awareness back to Samuel and his mother Elizabeth.

Katye: I am aware of how very tired Elizabeth is, the labor was very hard on her. It has always been of interest to me how labor being born and labor leaving the physical form upon death are much the same. It's like the soul knows upon entering the earth plane that it will leave its conscious connection with spirit, and sometimes this can be experienced as a difficult labor. Mother and child must be encouraged to do their sacred dance, just as the personality must be encouraged to leave the physical form during the time of transitioning back into the world of spirit.

I watch as the teams of physical and spiritual helpers continue to take care of mother and child. The doctor and nurses are unaware of the spiritual helpers that are helping the soul essence and baby units. No one seems to understand these first few minutes are very important as the soul essence and baby merge.

When mother and child are reunited I watch as Elizabeth holds her child. Samuel's father has just arrived at the hospital. As Elizabeth holds her baby in her arms, I hear her telling him that she will do her best to love and protect Samuel. The bond between this mother and child is a strong one. I watch as Samuel is taken away, for the doctor feels it is best for Elizabeth to get her rest. In 1953 the father was not permitted in the labor room, so William's first introduction to his son is through a glass window. While looking at his son, William offers a prayer of thanksgiving and dedicates Samuel's life to the glory of God. As he does so, William is unaware of the spirit helpers which surround his son and him.

I watch Samuel being poked and prodded by well meaning nurses doing their jobs. They too are unaware of the body of light which surrounds Samuel's physical body.

I watch in awe of the beings of light which surround Samuel. There appears to be light work going on as the physical baby sleeps.

Anna: Another pillar of conscious construction of the soul is "creation begins on the astral plane of consciousness but must be grounded into the physical earth plane once the baby is born. The divine blueprint of the soul must still be grounded into the physical." The spiritual beings surrounding Samuel will help to imprint and ground into Samuel's energy body the divine blueprint of that which the soul desires to create on the physical plane. This information will be contained in Samuel's earth star, however the blueprint will lay dormant until the personality liberates the energy of soul through life experiences.

Katye: Please expand this in more detail. This is a new concept for me, that the divine blueprint of that which the soul desires to manifest lies dormant within an earthstar.

Anna: The magnetic field is all encompassing, and it is this pulsating field of light which gives life to all. Think of the soulstar, earthstar and chakras as energy conductors of light energy, also known as life force energy. Chakras receive, assimilate and express the energy of the soul. The earthstar is a major receiving receptor of soul information. The earthstar holds the divine blueprint of the soul's life plan for its chosen incarnation. In the era in which Samuel incarnated, the human form cannot receive directly pure soul energy. The energy of soul must be grounded into Mother Earth and assimilated into energy that the human form can process without doing harm to the physical form. Mother Earth herself is a major receiver and conductor of universal life force energy. By grounding the energy of soul into the earthstar, Mother Earth symbolically cradles the life plan of the Soul until the personality is ready to bring forth the living plan of the soul.

Katye: This all sounds very complicated. How can Samuel or any incarnated being liberate the energy and plan of the soul if they are unaware that they are an incarnated soul?

Anna: Remember Katye, the soul will have ongoing connection with the incarnated personality through the magnetic field of energy which is in actuality contained within the living field of God. This web of light is a direct link to soul and the world of spirit. The magnetic field also connects all beings. Samuel's soul will also connect with the incarnated being through sleep time in the astral planes. Samuel's soul and spirit guides will communicate as the developing soul child grows in age through intuition. This is one reason many babies sleep so much during the first 6 months of life. The baby has a constant connection with soul during sleep time. The magnetic field of light strengthens the link between the physical and spiritual. Remember the baby is young but the soul essence in the case of Samuel is a very old one. Samuel's soul has fully anchored its soul essence into the infant child and will do what it can to ensure that its life plans are fulfilled.

Katye: I wish that others could see what I see as I observe Elizabeth getting ready to take her infant son home. They have spent about four days in the hospital and, although Samuel was in a nursery with other babies much of the time, Samuel was surrounded by his chosen spirit guides and his soul at all times. The infant child seems like it is adjusting to its surroundings and integrating the energy of the soul. I am just realizing what an amazing time this is for the incarnating soul as it begins to infuse the physical form with its soul essence. I can also see how watchful the spirit guides are with the child. It's almost as if there's a parallel experience going on, one physical and one spiritual.

I watch as Elizabeth is wheeled to the waiting car. She is holding her beloved son very tightly in her arms. As was the case during her delivery, Samuel's father is working on saving souls and he was not there to bring mother and child home. Elizabeth's father drives mother and child home. The ride home is in silence and allows Elizabeth to contemplate what is in store for her and her young infant. She has no conscious understanding of her soul contract with her son but she has an intuitive sense, a feeling deep within her gut that this may be the last time she and Samuel feel this deep bond.

Anna, I feel a deep sense of sadness in my heart because I know that the journey of Samuel and Elizabeth will indeed be a difficult one based on their soul contracts. I am somewhat comforted knowing that they will be supported by light beings, their souls and many others who have agreed to be that which they each need the other one to be to bring into fulfillment their binding and sacred soul agreements.

CHAPTER FIVE

EVOLUTION OF SOULS THROUGH EXPERIENCE

In this next section you will find what Anna likes to call discourses. This is generally the method she uses to teach. These discourses were given to Katye during the hours when Katye would normally be sleeping. Anna encouraged Katye and others to ask questions. Using this question and answer format Anna would bring forth the teachings. Anna also encouraged Katye to use her gifts of clear sight and traveling into the astral, causal and Akashic planes of consciousness to bring forth descriptions as experienced by Katye during many of the discourses.

We believe many of the discourses will have you asking more questions. Many of the discourses will challenge you because you have been taught to experience consciousness through what Anna calls physical consciousness.

Anna has stated that it is not a coincidence that they are bringing forth this information. The energies on many of the earth planes of consciousness have experienced a great shift since 2012. Personalities are ready to bring forth more of their divine selves.

We will pick up the journey of Samuel after the discourses. If you want to read what happened to Samuel go directly to chapter six.

SOUL PARENTING

March 9th 2014

Katye: Anna I have learned so much from you about children. In this discourse I would like to know how parents can begin to raise intuitive and creative children who stay connected to their soul.

Anna: First, let us state that everyone is born with intuition, which is a direct link to the guidance and communication with one's soul.

The sixth sense is not strengthened because the majority of parents and those in charge of the infant child have forgotten their own conscious link to soul guidance and communication. Children are encouraged to express the desires of parents not the desires of soul.

Katye: Would it be fair to say that parents do this unconsciously?

Anna: Of course, they do this unconsciously for the most part. Parenting is often an unconscious process. To raise creative, intuitive children, first, parents must bring forth the sacred truth that, no greater gift than this will one ever have.

Meaning this infant child, which inhabits the essence of soul, has agreed to entrust to you its formative years. The incarnated soul does not come to you to learn how to be an extension of you for it has its own goals, dreams and plans for its life. You have a soul agreement with this infant child. All soul agreements state that, "I will be that which you need me to be so that you can be that which you need to be." For the most part parents have forgotten this sacred agreement.

The creative process of the soul begins in the astral planes of creation. The incarnating soul trusts the chosen parents to care and nurture the child during its formative years. Depending on the life plans of the incarnating soul, many different experiences begin at birth.

We give you now a pillar of light which, if implemented on the earth plane of consciousness, would help to bring forth and ground the creative expression of the soul.

When a child is born all in attendance should pause and take a few moments to behold the wonder of that which has been created in love by a soul. God has now become individualized through the birth of this child; behold no greater gift than this.

A simple blessing: Behold no greater gift than this has been given. What we speak here is the gift of life, the gift of being an incarnating soul ready to begin anew its journey on the earth plane of consciousness.

Honor the creative force of soul which has now merged with the physical. And then honor the creative force of soul which dwells within you. Remember that within you is the spark of Creator God. All of those in attendance at a child's birth have just witnessed the miracle of spirit and flesh becoming united.

We remind you of the composition of the incarnated soul. At the severing of the cord, the soul sends forth the living spark of soul essence into the body of the newborn and, with it its energy bodies of light, begin to take shape and form. With each physical breath, the light bodies and the physical form begin to give birth to the spiritual manifestation of the soul.

The soul has created a physical life-form in which it will navigate the physical plane of reality. Once the union of physical and spirit have merged, the birthing process is complete. Life of the spiritual being begins with the severing of the cord. Once dependent on the mother for each breath, the child now begins to breathe on its own and, with each breath, grounds into the physical the essence of the soul which will experience life.

Please understand, Katye, although the incarnated soul inhabits the physical form of an infant, it has the direct influence of the soul. This soul influence continues as the infant goes through the biological and development stages.

Katye: Anna, what do you mean by, "Appears to be sleeping"?

Anna: We give you another pillar of light. The infant child's body is sleeping, however the infant child's light body is assimilating and assessing the environment which it has been born into. This information goes directly to soul. Souls understand that those around the incarnated soul during the formative years from birth to around age 6 or 7 will have great influence on what will eventually become the personality's vibrational signature.

Katye: I want to clearly understand what you are saying here. You are saying that the infant child, from the moment it's born, begins to monitor the environments into which it has incarnated.

Anna: Yes, this is correct. Understand, this is not a mental process, because the brain is still that of an infant child. The infant child through their energy field, mind and the constant connection to soul begins to understand energetically the environment into which it has incarnated.

Under ideal circumstances, the infant child sleeps allowing the physical process to unfold. The incarnated soul begins to fully assess the vibrations of the world into which it has been born.

Katye: I had no idea the infant child from birth was aware of its surroundings to this degree. You also said the infant child begins to develop its personality's vibrational signature. Could you please explain what you mean by this?

Anna: As we have stated, children quickly use their energy field to discover the world around them and, before they can even walk or talk, they have determined the lay of the land. Meaning, what do these other personalities expect from me? The soul and chosen energy companions help the developing child by reminding it that it was created for soul growth and expansion with dreams, goals and plans of its own. The energies of soul are comforting to the infant during this time of development. The pull to assimilate with those around them begins to pull the infant more and more into the waking state and away from the world of soul.

It is during this time that many parents reverse the process of soul parenting.

Katye: I have never heard of this term soul parenting.

Anna: We are aware of this. Soul parenting is a new term we give you now to help raise the consciousness of those who agree to be parents in the era of 2014. Soul parenting embraces the consciousness that the child is an incarnated soul with goals, plans and gifts which they have agreed to bring forth as a part of the soul agreements.

Those who raise the child and have connections to the developing child would do well to ask themselves, "What are my sacred and binding soul agreements and what am I to teach and learn from this incarnated soul?"

Remember, the developing child is highly sensitive to the environment around them and begins programming the beliefs of the tribe. The environment the developing child is exposed to begins influencing the vibrational signature of the incarnated soul. If a child is encouraged to bring forth the creative expression of the soul, it will begin to bring forth its own unique vibration.

Usually the developing child begins assimilating the vibrational signature of those around them. They do so to fit in, to belong to the tribe. Have no doubt, all souls understand this process of human development before incarnating.

The soul connection is on-going, as the incarnated soul goes through several stages of growth. We might add here, that these stages include energy influences from the soul. As the child develops its own personality, it will begin to be pulled toward the physical experiences of the tribe. Through the human energy field and what has been imprinted, the incarnated soul begins to grow and evolve. If the child is encouraged to express its individuality, a child will thrive and bring forth the creative expression of the soul.

As we have said, every child is born intuitive, which is a direct link to the guidance and communication with one's soul.

Currently this sixth sense is not strengthened because the majority of parents and those in charge of the infant child have long since forgotten their own link to soul guidance and communication. Children are not encouraged to express the desires of the soul. They are encouraged to express the desires of the parent or those in charge. Soul parenting understands that I have been entrusted to bring forth the creative expression of my child's soul, not to make him or her an extension of myself.

Katye: Wow, this, of course, is what parents who are unschooled about soul parenting do. They raise their children to adapt to their values, beliefs and for the most part think that their children are theirs.

Anna: Yes. This is a fallacy which we hope to change by this discourse. Children are a part of tribe and the incarnated souls who form the family unit have sacred and binding soul agreements. It would do well for those involved with the infant child to understand the incarnated soul, the child, is on their own journey.

Katye: How do we create a world, an environment, where the child will be encouraged to bring forth the creative energy of the soul? Anna, many children are born into tribes with beliefs set in stone in matters of religious expression, cultural norms and ethnic beliefs. How does the development of the incarnated soul fit in?

Anna: Every incarnated soul has carefully planned and chosen all of these influences as part of its life plan, however, we are seeking to bring forth teachings that the infant child is an incarnated soul which has chosen this environment and tribe.

The key to raising a child who is encouraged to bring forth the creative expression of the soul begins at birth. Those around the incarnating child need to understand that the child is an individual. This incarnating child has gifts, dreams and lessons to share and experience.

By understanding this, those around the child will begin to create an environment where the child is encouraged to express its individuality. This is where those who have agreed to be parents stray from soul parenting.

Those who agreed to be parents have agreed to put the needs of the developing child first. We understand, this is not the prevailing belief in the era of which we speak. Currently, parenting involves making the child adapt to the life the tribe had going before the birth of the child.

Parents and those around them try to shift the child into the structure that was created before the birth of the infant. Soul parenting means all those involved begin to attune and attend to the needs of the developing child. Soul parenting allows and opens space for the developing child to expand the consciousness of the tribe to create a new flow within the family unit.

Do you understand what we are teaching here? By allowing and opening space within the family unit for the infant child, parents create space for the infant to bring forth the creative expression of the soul. Instead of adapting to the vibration of the tribe, the infant child is encouraged to bring forth its own unique vibration.

All infants, being incarnated souls, bring with them, dreams, gifts and life lessons. Soul parenting creates space and allows the child to set their own pace. Some incarnated souls have trouble adapting to the physical form. Soul parenting allows for the developing infant to find its own rhythm in regards to the basic physical needs of the child. Be aware the basic needs of the child go far beyond sleeping, bathing and eating. The incarnated soul continues to have direct soul connection as well as ongoing help from its chosen spirit companions.

Soul parenting creates and allows space for the on-going soul connection. Soul parenting understands the infant child, although sleeping, is very aware of its environment. Soul parenting honors the on-going relationship between the world of spirit and the physical world of the incarnated child.

Katye: This all sounds wonderful, Anna, but how do we bring forth this new consciousness about soul parenting? Even those who are aware that their child is an incarnated soul do not create space for the developing child to expand the consciousness of the tribe. Learning on the earth planes of consciousness takes its toll on all personalities. The soul agreements seem so out of reach for most personalities.

Anna: We remind you that it is not the experience itself which is important to the incarnating soul. Experiences will change on the earth plane of consciousness. What does not change is the sacred and binding soul contracts agreed upon in the Hall of Records.

Through soul contracts, a parent has agreed to be that which the child needs him/her to be. In turn, the child has agreed to be that which the parents need him/her to be. Each chooses the other because the separate life plans would create an environment which would allow for the individual life plan of each incarnating soul.

Katye: So you are saying that, if personalities were schooled in the soul, they would see through the experience and embrace the life lessons as a means to an end, nothing more, and nothing less.

Anna: Yes. The personality schooled in soul would understand that the experiences are just that, experiences. Experiences themselves are not the reason for incarnating. The reason for incarnating is the same for every soul, which is soul growth and expansion. When one chooses to be a parent, one has agreed to create experiences which will help to bring forth the individual personality of the child. The personality may veer from the life path of the soul. The personality will be guided to experiences which will bring forth soul growth and soul expansion through on-going soul essence contact.

In truth, incarnating souls also know that, although the chosen parents will appear to have authority, there is truly no authority but that of soul and God consciousness. Soul essence contact will help the incarnated soul to understand, on some level of consciousness, that no matter what the experiences on the earth plane, all is well with one's soul.

Katye: Anna, you have spoken briefly about the needs of the developing child comes before the needs of the parents. Can you talk more about this?

Anna: We remind you that during the formative years of child development, the needs of the child are many. If a soul life plan includes being a parent, one has agreed to the enormous responsibility of creating an environment where the creative expression of the child's soul can thrive. You have heard the phrase, "It takes a village to raise a child." We would agree with this. This village, however, includes those of physical form as well of those in non physical.

Putting the developing child's needs first, means to create a world where there is time for the developing child to explore through all of their senses. This means patience, and allowing the developing child time to assimilate and ground the spiritual into the physical.

As you know, intuition is the first sense to be parented out, quickly followed by clear sight; smell and hearing are closely followed. Taste is really never developed beyond the taste of likes and dislikes of food and this again is according to those in charge of the growing child. There are many flavors to life, but the personality does not explore far past those adapted by the young child.

Katye: I've never thought that parents who love their children are responsible, for as you said, parenting out the use of the senses. Is there anything a parent can do to help encourage the child to fully develop their senses including intuition?

Anna: There are many things a parent can do. They can begin by creating a world where the child can thrive. By this we mean encourage them to be creative and create space where the child is encouraged to be sensitive of the surroundings around them.

As the child develops, bring forth your own creative expression. Learn to watch for cues from the developing infant. Even an infant will convey soul messages. Soul parenting understands that, although the physical form is developing, the soul age of the incarnated child may be one of a very old soul.

Katye: Anna, that's going to take a whole new level of consciousness for parents to even begin to understand and honor: that the developing child may be an old soul.

Anna: We would agree with this; however we believe that many are ready to embrace soul parenting. Soul parenting begins with the awareness that God has now become individualized through the birth of this child; behold no greater gift than this.

Another earlier discourse about soul parenting:
December 18th 2013
Anna on raising children in an unconscious world.

Katye: Yesterday I was talking to parents of an eight year old. They are very frustrated with their daughter and how needy she is.

Anna: We remind you the needs of the child outweigh the needs of the parent. By this we simply mean that during the formative years of child development, the needs of the child are many. If a soul life plan includes being a parent, one has agreed to the enormous responsibility of creating an environment where the creative expression of the child's life can shine through.

Katye: Wow! I wasn't expecting that statement. I have always believed that by taking care of self everyone in the family will benefit from it.

Anna: This is true, however, if one has agreed to be a parent, taking care of self must involve forming an identity with being a parent first and foremost. Understand, if one has agreed to be a parent, one has agreed to help the child bring forth the creative expression of the soul. Of course this is no easy task.

Keep in mind, the needs of the soul will be in choosing parents based on era, place, culture, and social standing to name a few of the choices a soul looks at before choosing its parents. Let us also remind you that many souls choose other experiences such as being raised in an orphanage. The journey of the soul takes one into many different experiences.

Katye: I am thinking about my children. I was a stay at home mom until they were eleven and thirteen, but I can't say I was conscious about much of my life, much less knowing that by having children their needs were first.

Anna: Katye this is still true for most parents.

Once a soul has chosen its goals for growth and expansion, it begins looking at who it will choose to entrust the formative years of childhood to. Every soul fully understands the era, place, culture and social standing will influence greatly the experiences of the child. Every soul who chooses to be a parent does so with the understanding that, during the formative years of the child, the parents will both put first the needs of the child. Currently this pillar of the soul is not a prevailing one on the earth plane.

You might ask here, "What are the needs of the child?" Of course there are many needs which are physical. The needs of the child are different depending on the desired experiences. What we are teaching here is a set of spiritual teachings on raising a child consciously, understanding that if you are a parent on the earth plane, this was decided before incarnating. This includes being a single parent, adopted parent, young parent, or an older parent.

The prevailing energy of parenting has been reduced to giving whatever energy is left over at the end of a very long day to the child or children. Souls understand this prevailing energy has existed for thousands of years. By the time the incarnated soul takes on the role of being a parent they have forgotten for the most part they have agreed to put their energy, time and attention on the child.

Everyone has parents but being a parent is a soul choice. The decision is often made on the earth plane unconsciously.

Katye: Did I agree in the astral plane to have my children when I was sixteen and then eighteen?

Anna: The date and time was agreed upon as a part of the soul agreement. To answer your question, yes.

Some souls agree to be your child to teach you, by being a guide. Some sign on to teach you by helping you grow through a change in consciousness.

Other souls sign on to journey with you as a good friend.

Rest assured all agreements between souls who come together to merge as a family do so understanding that many twists and turns might be experienced.

We are attempting, by this discourse, to bring into human consciousness what it means to have a sacred and binding covenant of being a parent.

A Soul chooses one's parents understanding that it will be giving those whom they chose for parents permission to make decisions for them during its formative years of childhood. Souls understand the many twists and turns life can take on the earth plane.

The choice of being born to an old soul age parent or a younger soul age parent is also considered by the incarnating soul.

You can see the thought and work which goes into the process of choosing one's parents on the astral plane.

As we have stated on the astral plane souls understand that if one agrees to be a parent one will be signing a sacred and binding agreement. The soul contract includes the needs of the child come first during the formative years of the child. This is not to imply that growth and expansion of the parent stops, quite the contrary in fact. Those who choose to be parents understand that by agreeing to be a parent it has agreed to put its focus and energy on parenting.

We understand that this concept of parenting has not existed on the earth planes for many thousands of years.

When a child is born parents would do well to ask themselves two questions. The first, how am I to serve you? The second, how will I teach you about love?

To be a parent, one must put aside one's childish ways of behaving and understand: there is no greater gift than that of being a parent. To serve a child means tending to the child's needs, physically, emotionally, and spiritually.

We would include the tribal experience plays a major role in parenting. Many grandparents and elders of the tribe depending on the era play a major role with the child. In the current era of which we speak, 2013, the importance of grandparents and elders of the tribe have been cast aside as an occasional visit.

If you are a parent, understand you have agreed to nurture and encourage your child to bring forth the creative expression of their soul. You can't do this if you yourself have not experienced your own creative expression of your soul.

Soul parenting involves creating an environment where the child is encouraged to explore without restrictions other than that of physical safety.

Soul parenting involves asking what this child needs from me? If every child's needs were the same parents would not learn very much now, would they?

When we are nurtured and encouraged by our tribe to bring forth our individuality as children the creative expression of our souls flourish. The goals and dreams of the soul are made manifest on the physical plane.

When the creative expression of your soul is guiding your life one begins to see the ebb and flow to life's circumstances. The personality understands the events and life situations are simply an outward manifestation of the human experience. One does not get lost in the experiences but uses them for soul growth and soul expansion.

Message to my parents from an incarnating soul:

As a soul I have watched you both grow. I already love you both very much. I chose the two of you to be my parents for many reasons. Leaving the soul plane is a choice. I know you both have forgotten the place I now call home but I am with God in a place souls experience consciousness between earth incarnations. You are with God in a place you call earth. As an incarnating soul I know I bring into your life a spark of Creator God which is within every sentient being.

To my mother I say thank you. I know the past few months have not always been easy on you. From the moment of my conception I have been connected to the developing fetus body which I will call my home while on earth. I am excited about being born and being born to the two of you whom I will call my parents. I have much to do and as a soul I have gifts, dreams and life lessons to bring to earth and to both of you. I will try very hard to remember that I am first and always a soul. While on earth I will have a physical body, but I am and will always be a spiritual being. Please as my parents help me remember this time that I am a spiritual being.

As a soul I already have consciousness. Although my body is new, my soul is very old. Integrating my soul with my physical body is a complex process. Only my body is undeveloped. My soul carries with it wisdom, and believes in love as the guiding force.

As your child I have already begun the process of connecting with both of you. In your wisdom you have understood that we are already connected. As an indwelling soul I know you both well. I am excited for our journey in the physical to begin.

As I hear the two of you in conversations I too am eager to begin our journey. I have waited for this time when our lives would begin anew.

Please know that I bring with me soul strengths and soul lessons. We will teach each other. We will challenge each other. We will watch each other grow together as a family. As my birth draws closer I am already drawing closer to the tribe I have chosen to journey with. I have much love to share and much love to embrace. I am ready. Soon very soon I will be born but before I am there will be the birth experience. I know you are both preparing for my birth. Please know we can plan but we must allow for events to unfold as they will. As a soul I know we can plan but then we must allow the process of life to unfold.

I believe this lifetime I will remember that I am an incarnated soul. I believe those around me will help me in doing so. Our soul agreements have been agreed upon in the Hall of Records. I promise to be that which you need me to be so you can be that which you need to be. May we seek to bring this sacred truth to life through the creative process of love.

I honor you. I am ready to leave this place of love for a place where many have forgotten that they are both created and creator. I come ready and excited for this gift of life on the earth planes of consciousness. I trust that we will bring forth the creative expressions of our souls and we will seek experiences through love.

Soon very soon, together we will journey.

Katye: Anna, if only that letter could be given to those involved with the incarnating soul. Perhaps someday, people like my granddaughter Kourtney will be present at the birthing experience. Personalities like Kourtney will be the ones to help those in attendance pause and begin the journey of the incarnated soul by honoring that which has just occurred. From the time she could speak, she said she wanted to be the one who held the babies after birth. She talked at the age of three about wanting to welcome the baby and to make them feel loved.

I realize now she understood, at the age of three, about creating space for the physical and spiritual to merge. Kourt is now in nursing school and she still wants to be the one to hold the infant child after birth. I have always understood that no hospital had such a position. Perhaps Kourtney will create the experience of creating space for the birthing experience to shift focus. This shift must understand the birthing process continues as the physical and spiritual merge.

Anna: Yes, Kourtney has been aware since early childhood that she is here to help shift consciousness about, not only the birthing process, but also about transition back into soul. You experienced her tenderness with John as he birthed back into spirit.

In the era of which we speak, a consciousness shift must occur to allow space for the birthing experience to change. This consciousness shift will occur when those of your granddaughter's generation begin to create a forum which will challenge that which is considered the norm for the birthing experience.

We leave you with this image of the future birthing experience.

When labor begins, those involved with the birth are informed. Whatever they are doing, they pause and connect with the incarnating soul. The laboring mother has chosen her physical team of those who will help her during labor. They gather around and begin to hold space for mother and child. Everyone is surrounded by their own team of spiritual guides. As the labor progresses the one who has been chosen to bring forth the physical child is honoring the dance of both mother and child.

The birth experience is a dance of both the child and the mother. The mother has prepared for the birth by learning how to honor her body. She has also learned the art of energetically shifting from the physical experience to the spiritual experience of birth. The spiritual process allows the mother to shift her energy from the pain of giving birth. The sacred dance between mother and child begins. Natural hormones are released into the mother's bloodstream which will allow the mother to slip into a trance like state.

Katye: I have never heard of the trance like state in childbirth.

Anna: Currently across the world, there is a remembrance of this experience of childbirth resurfacing. In the United States, your midwife movement is seeking to bring this remembrance; however there are many more who are seeking to prevent this from occurring. We will talk about this trance state and how to produce it in a future discourse.

We return now to the current discourse. Upon birth of the child, those in attendance create an environment in which spirit and physical are given space to continue the sacred dance of merging. By this we mean, they create an environment where the needs of the child outweigh the needs of the medical profession to get their job done and rush off to the next job. Bring forth into your consciousness that, surrounding the infant child, is a magnificent team of light beings. This of course is true for everyone in attendance. Although the physical birth is over, there is still much to do to successfully anchor the matrix of light which now surrounds the infant's physical body.

Dim the lights, play music that is soothing to the incarnating soul, speak softly, allow someone who is schooled in the teachings of the soul to hold the infant. Assure the infant that you understand that it is an incarnating soul. Honor the presence of the team of light workers in the room. Their job is overseeing the incarnating soul's light body and physical body are fully merged. We say unless there is a physical reason, allow time immediately after birth for the infant soul child to complete the birthing process of spirit. Those in attendance understand that although the physical birth is over, the birthing of the spirit continues as the light body merges with the physical.

It is important to understand that, from the moment of birth, the developing child is highly sensitive to the world around them. By creating space for the birth experience to include the spiritual the infant will begin its life fully embracing both physical and spiritual aspects of self. This of course is the first step into creating an environment which encourages the creative expression of the soul to shine through.

As the tribe began to gather around the incarnating soul, they should do so quietly and with reverence of that which has taken place. A soul has cast forth its spark of God into the infant child, and with physical birth the journey of the soul continues.

We remind you to honor the creative force of soul, which has now merged with the physical. And then honor the creative force of soul which dwells within you. Remember that within you is the spark of Creator God. When introduced to the infant soul, each member of the tribe, should reflect on the sacred soul agreements which were created in the astral realm and begins to unfold upon birth.

Remind yourself of the core of all soul agreements: "I will be that which you have asked me to be so you can be that which you need to be. May we seek to bring this sacred agreement into our experiences on the earth planes of consciousness as that which we have agreed in love on the astral planes of creation."

Katye: The experience of birth which you have just spoken about is such a beautiful experience. I look forward to others reading this discourse.

Anna: As with all of our discourses, we know this will inspire others to reach within and allow questions and this shift of consciousness to unfold.

Soul Contract
Soul contracts are created by souls in the astral planes. Soul agreements and contracts are entered into with holy alliance and with humble devotion. Each soul agrees to help other incarnating souls fulfill the desired life plan. Soul contracts include the agreement that each soul is connected and is dependent on each other to bring forth into the physical plane the life plan of the other souls with whom they have soul contracts.

Core Soul Agreements for Souls who choose to be parents include:

Souls chosen as a parent or guardian have agreed to the enormous responsibility of creating an environment where the creative expression of the child's soul can shine through. Soul contract includes, if one has agreed to be a parent, taking care of self must involve forming an identity with being a parent first and foremost during the formative years of the child.

Soul contract of a parent agrees to be that which the child needs him/her to be so the child can be that which he/she needs to be.

Soul contract includes that the key to raising a child who is encouraged to bring forth the creative expression of the soul begins at birth, with those around them understanding that this child is an individual and has gifts, dreams and lessons to share and experience.

Soul contract includes the agreement that parents or guardians will put aside one's childish ways of behaving, and understand there is no greater gift than that of being a parent. To serve a child means tending to the child's needs, physical, emotional, and spiritual.

Soul parenting involves creating an environment where the child is encouraged to explore without restrictions, other than that of physical safety.

Soul parenting understands the infant child, although sleeping, is very aware of its environment.

Soul parenting understands that the developing child's needs come first.

Soul parenting means when a child is born, all those involved begin to attune and attend to the needs of the developing child.

Soul parenting agrees to create a world where there is time for the developing child to explore through all of their senses. This means patience, and allowing the developing child time to assimilate and ground the spiritual into the physical.

Soul parenting understands that, although the physical form is developing, the soul age of the incarnated child may be one of a very old soul.

Soul parenting allows and opens space for the developing child to expand the consciousness of the tribe to create a new flow within the family unit.

Soul parenting creates and allows space for the ongoing soul connection.

Soul parenting honors the ongoing relationship between the world of spirit and the physical world of the incarnated child.

Soul parenting involves asking every day, what does this soul child need from me?

Soul contracts for the soul who will be the child: Each chooses the other because the separate life plans would create an environment which would allow for the individual life plan of each incarnating soul.

Those chosen as parents have agreed to create space for me to bring forth the creative expression of my soul. As my chosen parents / guardian I have agreed to give you authority over me during my formative years. I do so with the understanding that we both remember that the only true authority is soul and God consciousness.

In the hall of records, the souls who are incarnating gather together to seal together their chosen journeys. That which has been created in higher planes of consciousness with holy alliance and humble devotion must now be created in the denseness of the physical plane of consciousness. Each indwelling soul watches as the seal is placed upon the holy plan. It is with what humans describe as great excitement and energy inspired by the universal creative intelligence that the souls prepare to incarnate on the earth plane. When the chosen time arrives the soul begins the descent into the physical plane leaving behind soul family and those who remain in other planes of consciousness within Creator God.

As the baby takes its first breath, the soul projects a spark of its soul essence containing the codes of light and divine blueprint, which contain the chosen goals and path for its incarnation into the physical form it will inhabit during this lifetime. As the umbilical cord is severed, the light body of soul gently surrounds the body of the infant child.

With each breath the baby takes, it begins uniting with its soul. The heart which once beat through the physical connection to the mother now beats on its own. The umbilical cord has been severed. The cord of light connecting it to its soul is intact establishing an eternal connection with one's soul and Creator God.

Soul parenting begins with the awareness that God has now become individualized through the birth of this child; behold no greater gift than this.

Katye Anna

AUTISM IS NOT A CONDITION

January 23rd 2014

Katye: Through conversations with Anna I have learned that those who are being labeled autistic are a new race of incarnated souls. These incarnated souls have chosen to be born higher centering. They have chosen to incarnate knowing their personality will be diagnosed with the condition of autism. Souls know there is no "condition". This new race of incarnated souls will continue to come to planet earth. They understand the enormous job of birthing a new civilization. They also understand, choosing to birth this new race among personalities who have forgotten being incarnated souls will be difficult at best.

Anna's teachings about those labeled with autism are clear. These children are perfect the way they are. In the year of 2014 personalities are searching for answers that cannot be found within the medical community. Many searching for answers are those who are parents to this new race of beings. Their lives have been thrown upside down when they realize their child is not like other children. Fear sets in. Parents and those unschooled in the soul search for ways to change the child.

Anna can you please help us understand what is occurring? What are we to do to help this new race of incarnated souls? Why has this new race chosen to be so different?

Anna: First let us remind you that humankind has gone through many evolutionary changes. The human form has evolved from a body of light to the dense physical form incarnated souls currently inhabit. There have been several waves of souls who have agreed to participate in bringing forth this new race of beings. The first wave of incarnated souls was born during the early 1940's. The differences were more subtle. Parents and physicians were not as quick to diagnose and medicate. The odd social behaviors and limitations of the child caused parents to eventually seek help. They did not understand, nor do they understand in 2014 these children are perfect. These behaviors are not odd for higher centering personalities.

Katye: Anna you continue to say these children are perfect. They seem to have a whole spectrum of medical issues. They also have developmental issues, social issues and a whole range of behavior issues.

Anna: We can sense your passion. Katye the earth planes of consciousness continue to evolve. However the earth planes of consciousness embrace change slowly. Many of the social developmental issues are because of the demands placed on them to be " normal". The souls who have chosen to bring forth this new race do so knowing they are pioneers. These souls have chosen to bring forth into the physical dimensions of earth a new race which will be called homospiritus.

Katye: I was told several years ago that I was a homospiritus. Can you please explain?

Anna: Yes you are a homospiritus. Homospiritus simply refers to incarnated souls like yourself whose consciousness has shifted. This consciousness shift has expanded your ability to navigate between planes of consciousness at will. Homospiritus are moving away from the lower earth planes of consciousness and experiencing life on earth planes four and above. Energetically homospiritus hold more light in their energy fields as well as their physical form. The new race of which we speak will experience consciousness primarily on the fourth earth planes of consciousness and above.

Katye: What is the difference between someone like myself who has evolved into a homospiritus and the new race of incarnated souls?

Anna: Centering and the life plan of the soul.

Katye: Can you please explain what you mean by centering?

Anna: Centering is simply how the personality will react in a situation as well as the personality's primary automatic response. Centering is chosen by soul as a part of its life plan. The centers act as a communication bridge between the soul and the personality. Someone who is higher centering, sees both the world of spirit and the physical world. Being higher centering, soul essence contact is as natural as breathing.

Katye: Are these personalities always connected to soul? Do they have a direct knowing that they have this on-going connection with soul?

Anna: Do you have a direct knowing of breathing, it's automatic, and this is the experience for one who is higher center.

Again we remind you that those incarnated beings that have been diagnosed with autism are higher centering. Their goals are not like those who are being born creating experiences through all the centers. Of course even old souls go through the normal biological processes of those incarnating on the earth plane. The goals are different for those souls who choose to help birth this new race.

We might add here that those incarnating in the era of 2014 are being born with all their centers awakened. The souls who have chosen primarily higher centering have done so as their goal of helping to ground into the earth plane a new era of humankind. These souls have no need to experience childhood.

Katye: This is a very strange statement. Why wouldn't a soul want to experience childhood?

Anna: Remember Katye when a soul reaches old soul age it has experienced thousands of incarnations. Old souls choose to participate in the grand plan of birthing a new race. Of course not every old soul will choose to bring forth this new race. These old souls do not choose a parent to learn life lessons. They choose a soul for their parent who will help to birth the new race. All souls involved have agreed to participate in the grand plan before they incarnated.

We remind you again, souls who agreed to participate in the grand plan do so knowing that they are pioneers. Along with being born genetically different these children are born higher centering. Higher centering children do not lose their connection to the astral plane of existence. The goal of the higher centering incarnated souls is to bring back the phrase experiencing heaven on earth. These beautiful beings of light are sent forth by their souls to bring forth a new race.

As we have said the core difference between those who are being labeled as autistic and personalities like yourself is centering.

Children like yourself were labeled stupid and slow. The good news is you weren't medicated. Your wave of incarnated beings had centering from lower to higher and could fit in with what was considered normal. Your wave of incarnated souls understood it was not safe to talk about the world of spirit to which you were connected. These personalities fit in the box constructed for them by the education system of its time.

Let us also state that children who are diagnosed with ADD are experiencing life through moving back and forth between being higher and lower centering. These personalities are a part of the second wave of incarnated souls who are here to help birth the new race. This wave of incarnated souls found it harder to fit in than those of the first wave of beings. These personalities were born late 60's to early 80's. They hold a vibration of light that will help to ground the new race of incarnating souls. Many of these personalities will give birth to the incarnating souls who are bringing forth the new race. Many of these personalities have experienced feeling very separated and different. They are also known as star children.

Katye even you moved back and forth between the centers. Like many you felt different. You enjoyed your connection to the world of spirit. The trouble you experienced in school had nothing to do with your intelligence. You can remember sitting as a child in a classroom wanting to be as you described it as being out there with the angels. As a child you did not fit in because you were experiencing being a multi-sensory personality.

Many children who moved through the lower to higher centering became dropouts, castoff of the system. They often became addicts of some kind. They experimented with drugs. This was the first wave of souls who volunteered to change the planet. Many of these souls are the ones who are teaching a new way of life in the era of which we speak.

Now in the era and time of 2014 many of these misfits from the forties, fifties and sixties are opening fully their codes of light. These incarnated beings are remembering that they are incarnated souls. They are living in the light of their soul. Like yourself, this wave of beings have broken through the densest of the lower earth planes of consciousness. They have embraced the light of their souls, thus the term homospiritus.

The first wave of homospiritus are the ones who will help to birth a new era of humankind. This includes forging the way for these higher centering children. We realize much work lies ahead, however, Katye you are here to bring forth a new consciousness. The shift has happened and many of you have awakened the codes of light that will give birth to a new generation of beings.

Katye: I am filled with a sense of excitement and urgency in getting your discourses on autism in the hands of someone who has the power to help. I feel like I am called to be an emissary of light. We are giving birth to homospiritus and this means we are moving into a higher centering being.

These children are bringing back to the earth plane a remembrance of agape. We must begin the long journey of helping the parents, medical community, and teachers to understand that first and foremost there is nothing wrong with these children. We must also lay groundwork for how to protect these children. I understand as incarnated souls they have chosen this journey knowing that they are pioneers and the road they travel may be a very difficult one at best. I feel a sense of knowing and joy within me telling me that a little girl born in Spring Grove, Pennsylvania has been preparing for this day when she would bring forth the teachings of Anna. I have walked into my density as an emissary of light.

Many who are unschooled in the ways of the soul are the ones who diagnose autism.

Anna: Yes Katye, we have agreed to bring forth these teachings of light as a part of your soul's life plan. For many years you have received a steady stream of soul consciousness which you used to help change your own life and the lives of others.

The first shift in consciousness of humankind is to begin seeing these children as perfect just the way they are. They hold a vibration which is different but not flawed in any way. Their lack of what those around them call effective communication skills and focus is a part of their soul design.

They communicate much the way we communicate telepathically. Words are ineffective when trying to convey love. Love cannot be expressed by words but must be experienced by the heart. These higher center children are emissaries of light, sent forth to bring forth a new consciousness.

Many times when these children get upset it is because they have gotten pulled into the vibrational frequencies of those around them. Being telepathic these children sense the energy and hear the thoughts of those taking care of them.

Katye: Anna I must stop you here. You are saying that these higher centering children can sense the energy around them as well as know the thoughts of those taking care of them?

Anna: Yes, this is what we have said. Currently those who are the caregivers do not understand that they must take responsibility for the energy they are sending out via their own vibrational signature. This is one of the many gifts these higher centering children offer those on planet earth. When personalities begin to take responsibility for their thoughts they will begin to create experiences of love.

With every shift in consciousness the vibration of those who have agreed to participate must come into alignment. Thoughts communicate telepathically and create energy. Personalities who are higher centering are receiving one's thoughts telepathically. In turn they become a mirror for what they receive.

You have asked why children labeled with autism are so angry. They are mirroring the current vibration of the planet. They are mirroring the thoughts of their caregivers who have forgotten their soul contracts.

Remember Katye, if one is a parent to one of these children they have a soul contract to bring forth the creative expression of the child. Currently parents are not overjoyed when they realize their child is "different".

Currently many parents, teachers and physicians, unschooled in the understanding of soul see these children as flawed. These children are a perfect creation of love. They are old souls sent forth to teach those around them love. It's truly this simple. They are here to birth a new race. This race will return to the core teachings of love.

We remind you the reason for the soul creating an incarnation on the physical plane is for soul growth and expansion. Many personalities are unaware of one's soul. They are judging the human experience without fully understanding the genetic composition of the human form. Personalities see the new race as inferior.

Let us state here that what is being diagnosed as a social developmental issue is more about those involved with the child than the child. The incarnating soul has no need to experience the earth plane through what those on earth call social development. It would do well for parents and those involved with the child labeled autistic to ask what the desires of the incarnating soul are.

Understand the child diagnosed with autism has a rich relationship with other planes of consciousness. The souls who are choosing to incarnate knowing they will be labeled autistic are old souls whose goal is to help rebirth the remembrance of multifaceted existence on the physical plane.

The higher centering child has a rich existence with spirit. Those around the child want to make them lower centering. Eons ago souls began incarnating on the earth planes connected to their higher centers. Thus communication between soul and personalities was constant. This is true for incarnated souls who are birthing a new race.

Katye: I need to take that last statement in. You said being higher centering one has soul essence contact which is as natural as breathing, meaning it's automatic.

Anna: Yes Katye, we mean to infer that when one is higher centering one has continued conscious soul essence contact. Do you not have a continuing stream of higher light consciousness? Your transition into allowing this steady stream of consciousness has sometimes been difficult has it not? Many personalities like yourself turned away from your connection to spiritual consciousness. This is not an option for this last wave of incarnated souls. They remain higher centered.

This is one reason they seem to look off into the distance. These higher centered personalities are working hard to merge the spiritual and physical worlds. In a later discourse we will give more details of the inner world of this new race.

Pillar of light: Those schooled in the language of the soul would immediately know that a personality who has been born with a condition such as autism is an old soul. This old soul has chosen to participate in the birth of a new race.

HOW DO WE HELP

January 29th 2014

Katye: Anna, I understand that these children who are born and diagnosed with the spectrum of autism are birthing a new race. Knowing this does not help these children or their parents. I also understand everyone involved has a soul contract. Unfortunately most personalities have no remembrance that they are incarnated souls. I realize what is needed is a paradigm shift. I believe that many parents are ready to try anything. I also believe that most parents want their child to be a child who can smile, babble and fit in the demands of the world around them. Knowing this, how do we help these children?

I am reminded of the woman I met last year. I was asked to talk to her about conscious dying. When I met her I realized she didn't need my help because she was connected to the world of soul. She's an adult who was labeled autistic. I remember her telling me that around the age of eight she heard a voice say if she talked they would let her alone. I'm sure the voice she heard was her soul or guide. As we talked I watched her energy field and I could describe in detail her parallel life. She told me she had to learn how to focus, for example on the chair meaning to her the chair was not solid. I could "see" her focus was on the other world she was experiencing and this was the world of spirit.

As an adult this woman had energy that was very angelic. At least that is the way I described it. She said, "You people are trying to make us like you and we are not. You keep trying to make us experience the world through your lens and we cannot." Her words touched me deeply. I realized the truth of her words. I told her she didn't need help to return to the world of spirit because she had never left it.

She told me her surroundings needed to be minimalist. Meaning very simple and she responded best to black and white colors. This woman learned how to thrive in a world which did not encourage her to thrive. She learned how to live in a parallel world of spirit and matter. It was as natural as breathing her connection to soul and she didn't even have a name for it. She said it was just natural. I believe she was a first wave volunteer. Her soul chose to be born higher centering. She came here to open doors. She is a homospiritus. I have often wondered how she is doing. I would like to help her leave her physical body when the time comes for her to birth into spirit.

In keeping with this conversation I ask you, Anna, how do we help these children who are higher centering live among us? How do we change a medical and school system that is already archaic? How do we help parents embrace that their child is perfect and realized it's the system and expectations placed on them that are broken?

Anna: You are correct, Katye, a paradigm shift is needed. Before this shift in consciousness can occur we must help personalities wake up. You have asked what can be done for these children. We will now begin to refer to these children as higher centering, not autistic.

Stop trying to change them. They are a part of God's design and they are perfect. There is nothing wrong with these higher centering children. Remember, there is no "condition".

This is the first shift in consciousness which must occur. There is no "condition" except in the minds of those who are unschooled in soul.

The new race of incarnated souls who are higher centering have little desire to communicate with those around them verbally. They are, however, communicating through telepathy. This is how souls communicate on the higher planes of consciousness. It would do well for those around them to quiet themselves and work on remembering how to communicate in this manner.

Many of these higher centering beings are very creative and need an outlet for their creativity.

Remember this new race of incarnated souls is seeking to bring back to the earth plane a remembrance of agape. They are seeking to shift consciousness from physical consciousness to spiritual consciousness.

Higher centering childrens primary connection is with spirit. This is also true for homospiritus like yourself. This centering in what you call the future will be the norm for beings on the physical plane. You must understand the physical plane is still a planet of manifestation of soul. Eons ago higher centering was the norm. This was when souls first began to incarnate on the physical plane. Over time ten thousands of years as you call them in linear time lower centering became the norm. These lower centers, as you know, were primarily focused on survival and issues of navigating the physical plane in this manner.

Souls who chose to incarnate as higher centering have the same review and soul agreements as those who chose to incarnate as lower centering.

Going back to your question, these higher centering children want to ground into the earth plane the remembrance that the personality is an incarnated soul. As incarnated souls, these higher centered beings are emissaries of light. They are here to wake up the personalities on the physical planes of consciousness that they too are incarnated souls.

Understand, higher centering children do not lose their connection to the astral plane of existence. The goal of the higher centering child is to bring back the phrase, experiencing heaven on earth. These beautiful beings of light are sent forth by their souls to bring forth a new reality. A shift in consciousness will occur on the earth planes of consciousness because of these children.

As we have stated these personalities will be known as higher centering and homospiritus. The incarnating soul embarking on this journey in your era understands that being the pioneers there may be hardships. They understand they are incarnating in an era where most living on the planet have forgotten that they themselves are incarnated souls.

You are aware of the shift which occurred in December 2012. This shift was not experienced on a conscious level by those on earth planes one and two. Many like you did consciously experience the shift. It is no coincidence that the higher centered children are incarnating during the era. They understand there has never been a time on planet earth where the masses are ready for change.

Pillar of light: Do not spend one second pitying these children. They are connected to soul and things of spirit. No matter what the human experience, they know only love.

It would do well for parents to ask themselves what is the soul plan of this child. Ask what are our holy and binding agreements I have with this child? Your medical and educational systems are of no use to these higher centering children, because for the most part they are unschooled in the teachings of soul. Look what they have done to the first wave of pioneers sent forth over the last (earth time) 100 years and especially over the past 70 years.

To physicians we say, "Stop medicating these children!" You have participated in medicating generations of children which are simply higher centering. What your medication does is create a filter which begins to alter their vibration and their conscious connection and awareness of soul.

Physician, we say, when you focus on lack and disease your patients will honor you by giving you that which you desire. Admit you do not have the ability to help these children bring forth the creative expression of their soul. Reach within and bring forth the rememberance that you are an incarnated soul. Allow the stream of soul consciousness to fill your consciousness with why you chose to be a physician. You wanted to heal and help. Do you truly believe that you are healing the many? Medications heal no one. Begin to see these children through the eye of the soul. Begin to see all your patients through the eye of your soul. Your soul can guide you how to create miracles which will someday be normal as a new consciousness of health care emerges.

We say again. There is no condition such as autism. This was a label given out of frustration because higher centering children did not fit in the box.

Physicians, it is time to tear down the box. Connect to the creative expression of your soul. At the core you became a physician and swore an oath to do no harm. Begin to create effective change by admitting you do not know how to treat these higher centering children.

Take the first step and bring forth your inner healer. Connect with your own soul. Then and only then will you have the courage to stop medicating these higher centering children.

Change begins one incarnated soul at a time. Physicians be that change.

To teachers we say, stand up to the old ways and create experiences for all those who enter your classrooms. All children are unique individuals and it is your responsibility to bring forth the creative expression of their soul even in a classroom setting. The higher centering child cannot be taught in the current environment. As a part of your soul agreement you have the responsibility to stand in your own power and not allow those in authority to dictate. How many lives will it take for you to stand up to the dictators?

To parents we say, release the fear and disappointment that your child is not normal. They are not as many children around them. They will not respond to your internal need for them to perform for you. These children will not coo, smile and need you to cuddle them. Have no doubt, they are intelligent and creative. They are here to help humanity shift into a vibration of love. Yes, your child is different. All children are unique. You have a sacred and binding soul contract to be that which your child needs you to be, so he or she can be that which she or he needs to be. Begin to ask what fears you must release to bring forth not only your child's creative expression of his or her soul but also your own. You are a parent, advocate and protector of your child. You have a sacred and binding agreement to be a part of a consciousness shift.

You must use your voice to help bring forth change. You must protect your child from those who are not schooled in the teachings of soul. You must also shift your vibrational signature to one of love. This is the only energy which these gifted beings of light will respond to create change. Have no doubt, if you are smiling at these children but hold anything but love in your heart they will make it clear to you.

We understand your frustration and yes, your resentment. Everywhere you turn to for help usually leads to more frustration. Your cries go unheard. Turn to your soul and angelic guides. They have not abandoned you. You are not alone.

Your sacred contract is clear. You have promised to embrace the magnificence of your higher centered child. To do so you must embrace your own magnificence. Yes, there are many challenges. Begin to accept your higher centered child as perfect. They are a new race. You have been chosen to participate in this grand plan. Do not turn away from your higher centering child but embrace that you are part of a higher plan.

Your higher centering child has the great task of grounding higher streams of consciousness. They use the same physical body which all incarnated souls use in the era of 2014. This physical body is somewhat limiting. Souls who have volunteered to be a part of the grand plan understand this. Of course it is not until one has incarnated that the realities set in.

We would agree, many higher centering children are having trouble adjusting to this physical form. There is much you can do to help.

First, accept your higher centering child as perfect. See beyond the dreams and hopes your personality planned for this child. Allow yourself to remember your soul contract and the grand plan in which you have agreed to participate.

Many of these higher centering children are sensitive to your tainted food supply. Feed them only the highest forms of food and drink. Give them foods which will nourish their body. Stay away from genetically modified foods. Dairy is another substance which many of these higher centering children find difficult to assimilate into their bodies. Wheat is poison to many higher centering children. We would also remind you that the same foods and drink which poison these higher centering children are also greatly affecting others on your planet.

Most importantly, advocate for your higher centering child. Create an environment where he/she can bring forth the promptings of his/her soul. Learn the language your higher centered child speaks. Telepathic communication is the language which surpasses any language barrier.

Katye: Anna what can parents do with the outburst and anger?

Anna: Again, we remind you these children will mirror the energy around them. Many times when these children get upset it is because they have gotten pulled into the vibrational frequencies of those around them. Being telepathic, these children sense the energy and hear the thoughts of those taking care of them.

Take responsibility for your thoughts. Your higher centering child hears your thoughts. Being higher centering they do not take personal your disappointment that he/she is not like "normal" children. Own your emotions. Get help with your anger, disappointment and resentment.

Embrace the magnificence of your child. Together you are forging a new race. This race will be one grounded in love by incarnated souls who know only love.

Katye: I'm crying, my heart is heavy because we are so far away from this shift in consciousness.

Anna: Yes, in the era of which we speak this is true. However understand the shift in consciousness is taking place. Remember shifts in consciousness begin with one personality at a time, with one parent, teacher, physician at a time who brings forth the creative expression of their soul.

We understand that this discourse has only begun to touch the surface of the needs of the higher centering child. We ask those who read our words to ask us questions. This is the manner in which we teach. Our motivation for this discourse is to begin a dialog with others. There is much work to do, however we believe the masses are ready to embrace the truth behind our words.

ILLNESS AND CONDITIONS AS PARTOF THE SOUL LIFE PLAN

Katye: It's 4:35 and I'm so sleepy. I had a hard time getting out of bed. My thoughts are scattered. In my dream state I am aware that I kept dreaming about my sister Debbie. Her life, especially the last ten years, seemed so hard. When thinking about her, I think about the cancer that invaded her body. Anna, there are so many questions I have about disease and why there is so much pain and suffering on earth. This would seem to go against everything I believe about love. Why would a soul willingly choose to create a life where it knows the personality will suffer? I would like to understand, what purpose does sickness have in a souls' life plan, and when a soul is creating its life plan, does a soul plan to create illness such as cancer?

Anna: Katye, let us clearly state that a soul never chooses to create suffering. Suffering is created by the personality, never the soul. Suffering is an indication that an energy adjustment is needed. Remember, Katye, the reason for any soul incarnating on the physical plane is for the sole purpose of growth and expansion. When choosing an era, a soul is aware of the plague of that time. To answer your question, yes, many souls' life plan can include a life lesson such as cancer, but not for the reasons you might think.

We feel it necessary to make clear two distinctions concerning illness: The first distinction we make is disease which has been chosen by the soul before incarnating for the purpose of growth and expansion. The second distinction is disease experienced by the personality because it has created an energy system that cannot hold a vibration of health. This is because of the way the personality has integrated life experiences. This second reason for disease is an indication the personality is in need of soul essence contact as well as an energy adjustment.

We will begin with the first. As we have already explained, the incarnating soul has the resources of the universe available to it. When choosing an era, it is clear to the soul if there are any current plagues occurring during the time it will be on the physical plane. For soul growth, it may choose to participate in the plague of the era it is choosing. The soul is very aware that it is the personality who will have the experience of the chosen illness. However the personality is created solely for soul growth and expansion. Remember the soul is not limited to time, so it clearly understands in great detail what the personality might experience on a physical level. The soul is also very aware that, no matter how well one plans, it will ultimately be up to the personality how it chooses to cope with the disease. You yourself have seen many examples of how personalities cope with disease.

Katye: I still don´t understand why a soul would choose illness as a means for growth and expansion.

Anna: You are judging the experience of illness or health condition as a negative one. We remind you again the soul creates its life for growth and expansion and simply uses illness as an experience. The experience of illness or a health condition will be used by the soul to create many opportunities for growth. A soul chooses an illness or health condition based solely on the lessons provided by the illness. If the incarnating soul chooses to participate in a plague as a part of its life plan, it is doing so to bring attention to the health condition.

Please understand, illness such as the great plague of cancer is a manifestation of an unconscious world. A false sense of fear and separation has manifested the disease. The soul who chooses to knowingly participate in a disease does so in the hopes that it will help to change the energy which created the disease. All diseases begin as an unconscious belief of separation. There have been many eras where plagues did not cover the earth plane. There are many examples of people who cared for the inflicted and did not succumb to the illness. Ask yourself, "why"? Simply put, they did not hold the vibration of the disease within their consciousness.

When creating an incarnation, a soul can choose to encode within the DNA a program that will prevent the manifestation of the plague in the era it is incarnating into. Of course, this also means the soul can encode within the DNA of the incarnating personality's body the code that will allow the possibility of the disease to be created in the physical. The way the personality integrates experiences will determine if the code of the disease is turned on.

Disease does not manifest in everyone. Even if the personality is predisposed through genetics, this does not guarantee the disease and or condition will manifest. In truth, it is the personality whose beliefs turn on the genetic code. Of course what the scientific community is unaware of is the soul's involvement in choosing which codes to download into the physical structure of the incarnation.

Another pillar of the construction of the soul is that codes are placed within the DNA of the incarnating soul's body. The consciousness and beliefs of the personality will determine if the codes for disease are turned on.

Let us make clear here the incarnating soul's goal is never to manifest the disease in the physical. In choosing to participate in a disease/plague it is doing so as an opportunity to change the energy which in another lifetime it helped to create. It terms of your years on earth it takes many years for a disease like cancer to be created.

Another point of clarity: all disease is created on the physical plane. Soul creates only love. Every disease such as cancer, or any plague which runs rampant on the earth plane, was caused by a false belief of separation and fear. Souls, who choose to encode a disease into the DNA of the incarnating soul, have also downloaded the incarnating soul with the code that will create an energy adjustment. This energy adjustment will expunge the disease from the personality's physical and energy bodies. No medicine can do this. Energy which created the disease must be transformed. False beliefs which caused the plague to manifest in the physical must be transformed. The incarnating soul chooses to participate in transforming disease.

Do you understand what we are saying here? Soul does not want to participate in the disease. Soul wants to change the false beliefs which allowed the disease to manifest in the first place. Let us remind you again, that all disease is created from a false belief of separation and fear. For the disease to be eliminated, the belief which gave birth to it must be changed.

The soul, of course, understands what a great undertaking this is, for it knows that it will be the created personality who will have to choose which code to awaken. We repeat: the goal of the soul is never to create anything but love.

November 28th 2013

Katye: Yesterday, I listened to a recording we made of Anna. I must admit I feel a kinship with her. Although Anna is nine hundred seventy-six souls strong, the energy behind her voice is beautiful. I am in awe of the love our soul families have for us. While traveling on the earth plane I know many personalities feel separated. We are so loved.

Yesterday, Anna introduced the term "energy adjustment" as well as the encoding of disease into the created personality's life-form. I would like to continue learning more on these topics if Anna feels this would be helpful.

I am aware of being guided to breathe deeply. I know I am preparing my body for the energies of Anna.

Anna: We have stated before, physicians need to be educated in matters of the soul. Placing one's health in the hands of someone who merely looks at the presenting illness and outward symptoms is foolish at best. The law of the universe is simple: what you focus on you will create more of. Physicians unschooled in the soul who focus on disease cannot create health for their patients. We spoke to Allan yesterday about medicine that many on the planet are taking. In many patients medicine causes more harm than good. We know these words are strong, however, many of us have had lives as healers and physicians and we desire to change the energy we have helped to unleash on the physical plane. Physicians take vows to do no harm. We know most physicians believe they are helping their patients. However, one cannot treat the physical body and neglect the care of the soul.

Katye: Anna, you aren't telling people not to take medicine prescribed by their doctors?

Anna: No, we are not. When you introduce chemicals of any kind into the physical form the body begins to chemically change itself and becomes dependent on the medication. We are simply saying that, with every medicine introduced into the physical body, the medication begins to alter what soul has created. When you introduce a medication into the body, the body must now adjust to this new energy. This in turn begins to alter the flow of the body as well as the energy field of the personality. Man-made medications do not take into account the ripple effect they will have on not only the chemical structure of the physical form, but also the ripple effect it will have in the energy field. With each medication introduced into the physical form, more adjustments must be made by the body .

Be clear, medications do not heal the illness. Medications simply mask the presenting illness. We will say again, putting one's health into the hands of a healthcare system unlearned in the teachings of soul is foolish at best.

Because you are an incarnated soul, the physical body and mind must be cared for multidimensionally. Meaning there are many levels to the care of the incarnated being. Physicians untrained about soul will have no understanding if the presenting illness is in alignment with a chosen life lesson of the soul. They will be confused if the presenting illness and/or condition is a result of the personality having created an energy system which cannot hold a vibration of health.

A physician schooled in teachings of soul would understand that any disease is an indication that soul essence contact is needed. Soul essence contact will determine if the personality is creating the illness. Has the personality awakened a code which had been downloaded by the soul before incarnating? Is the presenting disease a result of the personality having created an energy system which cannot hold a vibration of health? These are questions a physician schooled in the soul would ask.

Katye: Anna, how would a physician know if the illness is a part of the soul life plan or a manifestation of the personality.

Anna: The answer to this question is not a simple one. We will attempt to bring forth some clarity. Two distinctions we can give you; major diseases and/or conditions such as Down's Syndrome and childhood cancers in children are always a part of a soul's life plan. We will talk more about childhood illness in a later discourse.

Remember, the soul chooses which codes to encode into the DNA. It is the total life experiences which opens the code from the DNA, be it for health or for disease. When an incarnating soul's personality has ongoing soul essence contact it creates health. The body is designed to know only perfect health. Patterns of health and disease have been established before adolescence. Keys within the human energy field begin to slowly turn on the codes for disease/illness or health.

Katye: Anna, what do you mean by patterns of disease?

Anna: We use the word pattern simply to define repetitive behaviors and/or modes of response which for the most part are unconscious. By adolescence these unconscious responses begin to form the way one behaves in the world and sees the world. The unconscious responses begin to determine if a disease downloaded into the DNA will be turned on or not.

Simply because a disease has been keyed and turned on does not mean the personality will experience an onset of symptoms immediately. When symptoms are experienced, this is the time to connect with one's soul. The personality who has knowledge of being an incarnated soul will understand symptoms are an indication that soul essence contact is needed.

Understanding that a disease or condition is in alignment with the soul's life plan physicians could work more effectually. One would do well to understand that the incarnated being is an old soul who has chosen this experience. Take, for example, children with Down's Syndrome. These children are angelic by nature, and their life plan includes teaching others in this way. Choosing a body and or condition with limitations was a soul choice. Souls use this form to be of service to the greater good.

The creative expression of the soul is not being blocked simply because of physical heath. Much to the contrary, these enlightened souls are giving others an opportunity to grow. They have included as part of their life plan the physical form which others often shy away from.

As for disease and health patterns brought on by the personality due to the experiences of life, a doctor schooled in the knowledge of soul would understand that soul essence contact is needed.

When an incarnated soul's personality has ongoing soul essence contact, it creates health of body and mind. The creative expression of the soul shines through. Patterns of health are established.

When one's soul is guiding one's life, one begins to see the ebb and flow to life's circumstances. The personality understands the events and life situations are simply an outward manifestation of the human experience. One does not get lost in the experiences but uses them for soul growth and soul expansion. Many personalities turn life experiences into unconscious beliefs. Unconscious beliefs create patterns of fear, despair, guilt, shame and so on. These emotions create a breeding ground for the disease process to be turned on.

When symptoms present themselves, this is the body-mind signaling that soul essence contact is needed. By bringing these truths into one's awareness one can begin to make a consciousness shift and open a pathway for the Soul to shine through.

We will now begin our discourse of what we mean by energy adjustment. We introduced this subject in a discourse about disease and thus health. We are passionate about many subjects, however we believe when those in physical form understand that, it would do them well to embrace this major teaching of light.

We would tell each one of you to try our methods of healing the physical form in small areas of your life. When you see results then we would suggest you use more of the methods we teach.

The steps for energy adjustments begin with the personality contacting the soul. Unlike your physical doctor, soul is always available. We will use the analogy of the steps one takes with their doctor. When presented with an illness, one generally calls and makes an appointment with their doctor. At this appointment they tell the doctor what is occurring, meaning they describe the symptoms they are experiencing.

We would direct you to do the same with your soul. Communicate to your soul what you are experiencing. Using Allan and his health, he would simply state to his soul his health issues and concerns. Doing this, Allan is getting the attention of his soul. The soul has not abandoned the personality. It must be made known to soul that the personality desires help. Remember, the soul has many on-going alternative realties as well as continuing its own path of growth and learning. Most personalities go to the doctor for this help. It is a waste of time to put one's health in the hands of anyone who isn't educated in energy structure of the soul. Medicine and surgery cannot heal the illness. It can only lay at bay the presenting symptoms. The human body must be cared for multidimensionally, meaning there are many levels of care of the incarnated being. The doctor who does not take into account the entire composite of the incarnated being is doing more harm than good. Those who have forgotten they themselves are a soul cannot treat the soul of another.

Katye: I have met many loving and well meaning doctors. They work long hours.

Anna: Yes, when we were in physical form many of us were those well meaning and loving doctors. physicians and those in the healthcare system would do well to work less and meditate more. We do not mean to infer that physicians in the current healthcare system do not care. However we do mean to infer that they have forgotten how to heal. Ridding patients of symptoms is not healing.

We now give you instructions on Soul Energy Adjustment. Soul energy adjustments bring the physical and spiritual elements of the soul's plan into alignment with the physical incarnation and experiences.

SOUL ENERGY ADJUSTMENT

Step One: Contact your soul: communicate to your soul what you are experiencing. You can do this by writing, or simply talk to your soul, telling your soul about the issue/issues.

Keys to opening the flow of energy from soul are HEARTFELT COMMUNICATION followed by PERMISSION along with OPENNESS and WILLINGNESS to have the soul energy adjustments.

Energy adjustments of the soul must be in alignment with the will and desire of the personality to open oneself to the needed energy adjustments.

When asking for an energy alignment, one is asking the soul to open the code for health as well as to bring your life and body back into alignment with the goals and desires of the soul. If the creative expression of one's soul has been blocked, when energy adjustments are asked for, one's life will change to be in alignment with the soul's plan.

Step Two: You have communicated with soul and asked for help. You have agreed to bring into alignment your life with the desires and plans of your soul. Now simply allow time to RECEIVE the energy adjustments.

We would suggest you lay or sit down for at least fifteen minutes two times a day. (thirty minutes if time allows.) Begin by taking deep breaths and simply open your entire being to receive soul essence energy and adjustments.

The process of soul energy adjustments is mutidimentional. Meaning your energy field, chakras, physical form and mind will receive energy from your soul. Your spirit guides will also work on you during this time. Understand, being multifaceted, you have always had a team of spirit helpers with you. The shift in consciousness is, you are now aware of their help. With each energy adjustment the experience will expand. Eventually your consciousness will expand to allow you to fully experience your spiritual guides working on you during your energy adjustments. Enjoy, receive and embrace the truth that you are opening to the truth of being a multidimensional being.

During the time you are receiving the energy adjustments, it is best to get out of the way. This is the time you open up to receive soul essence energy. For many of you, in the beginning of this consciousness shift this will not be easy. If your cluttered mind gets in the way, simply tell it to be silent.

As you take time everyday to allow for soul essence contact, you will begin to notice changes in your life, be it physically, emotionally and/or spiritually depending on the area of focus for the adjustments.

When you are finished with your energy adjustment session, simply thank your soul and spiritual guides.

Step Three: Accept responsibility for that which you have created.

Another code of light is that, upon asking for a soul energy adjustment, it is up to the personality to begin grounding the desired change into the physical plane by their CHOICES. It is now a choice to allow the creative expression of your soul to shine through the experiences of your life or to continue living unconsciously. With each energy adjustment your consciousness will expand allowing for more of your soul to shine through.

Asking for energy adjustments and continuing to make choices which created the imbalance one is simply not taking responsibility for that which it created. You must change your life. Open up and allow the energy of your soul to fuel your life.

Practice releasing old outdated beliefs and patterns every day. To do this you must place focus on your growth NOT on the areas of your life which are stagnant. Begin by observing your life. Identify what patterns and archetypal influences are currently affecting your life experiences.

Begin to practice spiritual discernment.

Begin to notice in what situations and with whom you move away from your truth and guidance. When you do this, you are blocking out your intuition, guidance from your soul.

Affirm: I AM THE ONLY AUTHORITY IN MY LIFE. Invoking this truth you begin to claim that your soul is the only authority and guide you seek for guidance. Yes it's normal to seek guidance from others but in the end the only guidance which is to be followed is the soul. Your soul is connected at all times to love and to Creator God.

Permitting others' beliefs to have authority over you is now a choice. Permitting old patterns, experienced losses, hurts, and harm done to you by others and life experiences to continue to have authority over you is a choice. One must claim mastery over one's mind. Reclaim your birth right to create your experiences through love and with the understanding and knowledge that every life experience has many variables to them.

Remember within you is the spark of God. Create as God would have you create through love.

Practice affirmations everyday which will help to ground the energy adjustments:

Affirm: I listen to and follow the guidance of my soul. *Affirm:* I practice spiritual awareness and discernment at all times. *Affirm:* I embrace the creative expression of my soul in every area of my life. *Affirm:* My body knows only perfect health. *Affirm:* I commit to a daily practice of soul energy adjustments. *Affirm:* Creator God is individualized through me. Creator God enjoys being me. My soul essence has traveled the many planes of reality within Creator God.

Affirm: From this day forward I live as a being of light. I love being in a human body and love being on Mother Earth. I am an enlightened consciousness of Creator God in a physical body. My soul essence shines through my life.

I embrace multidimensional living. I know how to navigate the many planes of existence that are within Creator God, and I know that through focused pure intention I can direct my consciousness to any plane of reality at any time.

I give birth to all that is Divine, Pure and Holy. I have reverence for Mother Earth and all her inhabitants as well as the many planes of existence within God. I embrace my multidimensionality.

I affirm that through focused, pure intention and for the healing of all, I connect with the consciousness of pure thought, mind and love. I embrace my multidimensional beingness and I remember.

ANGELS AND SPIRIT GUIDES

March 31st 2014

Katye: Yesterday we had our first family gathering. It was wonderful working with children from age six to twenty-four. I realized that many of these children and young adults have no clear understanding about the many spirit guides they have in their lives. In my own life, no one ever talked about angels and spirit guides. I understand through my work with you, Anna, how my spirit guides came with me on this journey we call life to help guide, teach and encourage me to bring forth the creative expression of my soul. Anna, you have taught about the ongoing influence of soul and that our souls choose spirit guides to journey with us every step of our lives. I believe part of our work is to help children, and those who journey with them, to begin to understand the sacred relationship we have with spirit guides.

I can remember my spirit guides being with me as a little girl. I understand that we all have ongoing connection with our soul and spirit guides during the formative years of our lives. I also understand that my relationship with my spirit guides was not something I shared with those around me.

I remember sitting in first grade looking out the window. I wanted to be "out there" with my angelic companions. I found it difficult at best to focus on the mundane task of learning reading and arithmetic. Even in the 1950's the school environment did not help to bring forth the creative expression of my soul. I clearly remember Mac, my angelic companion, encouraging me to focus. I believe this is why I spent two years in first grade. It wasn't that I was slow, or stupid as my peers called me. I just found it difficult to focus and sit all day. Before going to school I had spent my time free, free to connect with the world of spirit. School made me focus on things I had no desire to focus on. As a little girl who didn't fit in, I found comfort in my "friends" that no one else could see.

I remember being at my grandfather's funeral. I was nine years old. When I walked into the church and saw his closed casket, I remember being very confused. I could see the grief and sadness that was all around me but I was also very aware of all the light beings. I could still feel this man that I called grandfather. I remember seeing souls hovering around those in mourning. As I looked into the church, I could see light beings surrounding my family. Everyone was so sad, and they were not able to see the beings of light who were everywhere. As I grew up, I remember going to other funerals and the experience was always the same. Grief everywhere, however the spirit guides were doing their best to console those grieving. I remember many years later at my sister-in-law's funeral, my granddaughter Kourtney said, "Grandma, do you see them? They are everywhere." She of course was referring to all the angelic beings see was seeing.

Anna, you have said many times that spirit guides and our soul cannot intervene unless the personality asks for help, and if it's in alignment with our soul's plan. I remember being 13 years old and I had a lump in my breast. Surgery was scheduled. I was relaxing by the pool and looking up at the sky connecting with my angels. I know I was scared about the surgery and was talking to the angels. Suddenly, I remember this heat moving through my breast as the most beautiful angel I had ever seen seemed to engulf me with her love. I'm not sure how long this continued, but I remember later going to my mother and telling her I didn't need the surgery, that the lump was gone. I don't remember telling my parents about what had just happened. Needless to say, the lump was gone and the surgery was cancelled. I now understand that I received a soul intervention. I'm assuming now that the lump and the surgery was not a part of my soul's life plan and therefore the healing occurred.

It seems shortly after this that my personality began pushing my spirit guides into the confines of my mind. It would not be until my 40's that I would consciously embrace my spirit companions again. In fact, it was through my spirit guides that I found my way back to my soul again.

Now, writing this book, I begin to remember the many times in my life that my angelic companions and my soul helped guide my life. Anna, how do we help people remember that everyone has spirit guides and that the imaginary friends children have are indeed spirit guides and companions chosen by their soul?

Anna: Thank you for sharing a few of your experiences. Through our discourses you have learned that a soul carefully plans its incarnation. Souls know that the earth journey is one where the incarnated soul, no matter how old it may be in soul age, must inhabit the form of an infant child. Souls are aware the earth plane is a plane of consciousness where the incarnated soul finds it difficult to maintain a relationship with the world of spirit. As you are well aware, the incarnated soul must go through stages of human development. Theses stages of development run the course which has been deemed as normal for the developing child. The majority of personalities on the earth planes still focus on physical consciousness instead of soul consciousness. Soul consciousness, of course, includes honoring the physical experiences but also honors the way of the soul.

Currently in the era in which you reside, this human development does not include, for most children, teachings that they have spirit guides, much less that they are incarnated souls. For this reason, each soul, with the aid of the higher counsel, chooses several spirit guides to accompany the incarnating soul as a part of their pre-birthing plan.

Upon creating the incarnation, the soul carefully chooses spirit guides. These spirit guides will not only communicate with the personality, but will alert the soul to anything that threatens the life plan the soul has chosen for the incarnation. You have asked us to explain about angels because they have played such an important part of your journey.

First, we want you to understand, Angelics have their own path. They are vibrational beings who have had a very long association with souls who are on the reincarnation cycle on the earth plane. Remember also, that as a soul grows and expands its own consciousness, it also expands the awareness of other planes of existence, including those outside your solar system. Angelics come from a higher plane of consciousness within Creator God. Many spirit guides are from other planets. Because many on the earth plane have forgotten this association with other beings, spirit guides have been reduced as an occasional association for the few when needed. A relationship with one's chosen spirit guides is one of the most intimate relationships one will have while on the earth plane.

These emissaries of light have chosen to participate on the earth plane by being guides. There have been many different vibrations of spirit guides focusing their energy and consciousness on the earth plane. In keeping with the holy alliance one has with other incarnating souls, one also has a holy alliance with spirit guides.

We would like you to understand that, although you have a strong association with Angelics, there are many other vibrations of spirit guides. There are many different kinds of spirit guides. You have a spirit guide known to you as grandfather dolphin. This spirit teacher taught you throughout your life, has he not?

Katye: Yes, grandfather dolphin takes me into the depths of the sea. He has been an active guide for the past twenty years or so. I have also had guides known to me as ascended masters. Master DK, Mother Mary, Jesus and Mary Magdalene have been teachers of light for me.

Anna: Mother Mary, Jesus and Mary Magdalene were spirit teachers chosen for you by your soul. Your soul chose the path of Christianity for you in this incarnation. Because of this, these guides which are associated with Christianity were chosen. Your relationship with Jesus has gone through many cycles of growth as well as lifetimes.

Katye: This is true. I have not been a practicing Christian for many years, however these spiritual guides continue to guide me in the path of love. I embrace what is known to me as Christ consciousness, the way of love. Master DK is a spiritual teacher from the Buddhic plane of consciousness. I have been aware of his presence during the past twenty years on a conscious level. I understand now that Jesus, Mother Mary and Mary Magdalene journeyed with me because my soul's life plan included being raised by my parents as a Christian. Long after I left the church, these spirit teachers taught and inspired me to bring forth love. In truth they taught me the way of love by choice.

Anna: Yes, these spirit teachers now serve humanity from the Buddhic planes of consciousness. They are spirit guides and teachers. What we are conveying here is how everyone's spirit guides are chosen for them, depending on the chosen path of your soul. Spirit guides and spirit teachers are known by many names in every culture. Currently in the culture and era your personality resides in, most have no conscious awareness of their spirit guides and spirit teachers.

A soul chooses spirit guides and spiritual influences knowing that the personality may or may not have a conscious awareness of the guide. As part of its life plan, soul has chosen goals and desired lessons for soul growth and expansion. Each soul selects spirit guides whose vibration will be helpful to the personality during the course of its incarnation.

Katye: I remember you teaching in another discourse how our spirit guides actually project their light essence through our energy field.

Anna: Yes, this is correct. The incarnating soul chooses spiritual guides who will radiate in one's energy field the energetic influence of the vibration of the chosen guide. Spirit guides have bodies of light that vibrate at different frequencies. These frequencies also includes spectrum of light rays which radiate into the energy field of those they travel with.

Spirit guides are comprised of many different attributes and energies. Qualities and attributes include: wisdom, patience, loving, joyful, guidance, peacefulness, strength, humor, tranquility, acceptance, insight and unconditional love, to name a few.

Spirit guides are dedicated to bringing forth the divine plan of the soul. The relationship between spirit guide and soul is one of divine love. The plan of the incarnating soul is the ONLY focus for the spirit guide. Spirit guides have no desire other than helping the soul's life plan to be fulfilled on the earth plane. Other than one's own soul, Angelic spirit guides are the most intimate relationship a personality can have, on the earth plane of consciousness, or any other plane. Therefore, a soul will choose many different spiritual guides who will journey with the incarnated soul through the course of the life experiences.

Katye: How do we teach children about their spirit guides?

Anna: As we have taught, every infant has ongoing connection with their soul and spirit guides during their formative years. Parents, teachers and peers have, for the most part, forgotten their own connection to soul and spirit guides, thus focus on physical consciousness. We seek, through our teachings, to bring the way of the soul back into parenting. To do this, those surrounding the infant must bring into their own consciousness the way of the soul.

Katye: Well, that's not going to be an easy task.

Anna: Yes, this is true. However many are ready to bring the teachings of soul back into the consciousness of the "human" experience.

To bring forth a conscious remembrance of spirit guides, it would be helpful to first bring forth a remembrance that one is an incarnated soul. As personalities begin to embrace that they are incarnated souls, they will begin to search for teachings of the soul. These teachings have been forgotten and or lost.

Personalities must begin to reconnect with their own intuition. Intuition, as we have taught, is guidance and communication from one's soul. As intuition is strengthened, communication with the world of spirit is also developed.

We have spoken in our discourse on soul parenting that, from the moment of birth, soul parenting embraces the incarnated child as spirit made manifest in the physical. Soul parenting includes honoring the incarnated soul's ongoing connection with spirit, and creates space for the developing child to bring forth the creative expression of the soul. Soul parenting helps the child ground the ongoing connection with soul and spirit guides. Simply talking about being an incarnated soul and creating space for the developing child to talk about his/her spirit companions strengthens the connection with soul consciousness.

A simple reminder at bedtime around the age of three that while the child's body sleeps he/she will travel through its beautiful body of light into the astral planes. Astral travel during this age is kept very simple. The child may be an old soul and will understand this while in the astral planes. Spirit guides travel with the incarnated soul during astral travel. When saying goodnight simply affirm that Susan's spirit guides will continue to watch over Susan as her physical body sleeps.

Spirit guides also surround the physical form while the body is in sleep state. We would suggest with young children you simply tell the young child that their spirit guide is with them at all times. Upon waking, parents can help the child ground the astral time and dream time by simply encouraging them to talk about their dreams. Parents can also encourage the child to talk about his/her spirit guides. By the age of six, it should be instilled in the developing child that physical and spiritual consciousness are a combination of who they are.

Katye: What you are guiding parents to do is very different. I don't know of any culture which encourages astral travel, dream time, and spirit guides playing an active role in a child's life.

Anna: Yes, currently on the earth planes of consciousness, physical consciousness is the norm. However since the shift, many are ready to bring forth these teachings. You have seen children in your first family gathering, have you not, who are as young as nine years old, who are talking about angels and hearing music?

Katye: Yes. I was thrilled to help these children begin to embrace that the sounds that they hear is the way their spirit guides communicate with them.

Anna: During your family gathering, you helped the young children understand, when they hear music which those around them don't hear, their spirit guides are sending them a message that they are with the child. Teach the children to use this spirit connection to help them understand that their spirit guides are letting them know that they are not alone. The parents who brought their children yesterday have some understanding of the ways of soul, but have not reconnected with their own spirit guides and teachers. Their children are helping them remember their own soul connection.

Katye: Yes, I clearly saw that the children have integrated a vibrational signature which is different from the tribe.

Anna: Yes, they have succeeded in creating a vibrational signature which is, in effect, helping those around them wake up. As we have mentioned earlier, souls choose spirit guides for several reasons.

Two primary reasons are:

One, the incarnating soul has chosen experiences in which the vibration and guidance from a particular angelic influence would be helpful to the personality.

Two, the incarnating soul wants to have a certain angelic vibration in the personality's energy field. The sole reason for this is to radiate in one's energy field the energetic influence of a certain vibration.

As with the young children who came to your circle, they have adapted a vibrational signature which radiates love. The young girl Maddie's vibrational signature has helped her two mothers seek the world of soul. Although new to the ways of soul, these young parents are creating an environment for their old soul daughter to thrive.

In moving forward, we encourage personalities to embrace the teachings that all personalities are incarnated with a team of spirit guides. This team of spirit guides changes through the course of one's life. The definition we use for spirit guides includes those of non physical form whose desire and goal is to be a participant on the physical plane. Spirit guides desire to help the incarnated personality navigate the incarnation. Spirit guides may have many forms and come from many planes of consciousness, including those from other planets. Each incarnated soul chooses many different guides which can include spirit guides in the form of what is known as a totem animal.

Invite your spirit guides into your life. Welcome them by acknowledging their presence. Simply say, "My heart is open to receive the gifts, energy, assistance and guidance of my spirit guides. I welcome your presence into my consciousness and my life. Please make your presence known to me. Please teach, guide, direct, inspire and help me connect with my soul. I open my heart. I am consciously ready to receive your gifts of healing, inspiration and love."

Take time everyday to open your life and your heart to your spirit teachers and guides. Embrace their presence in your life and acknowledge them as you would anyone you loved. Remember, these spirit guides and teachers serve humanity with humble devotion from the Messianic Plane and the Buddhic planes of consciousness.

Create time everyday to consciously connect with your spirit guides and teachers. Open your heart and bring into conscious awareness the way of the soul.

You were created in love. Your soul chose spirit guides and teachers who would greatly influence your life, consciously or unconsciously. Begin today to embrace soul consciousness and bring the love and guidance from the spirit world into your life.

DREAMS AND ASTRAL TRAVEL

December 22nd 2013 4:00AM

Katye: Anna, I am beginning to understand just how much influence those in the astral plane have influenced and guided my work. I have known for years that I wake up with inspiration and that everything we taught came from the realm of soul. I now have a greater understanding that I am and have always been a traveler. Meaning going out to the astral plane every night is as normal for me as what I do during the times I'm awake.

I'm beginning to understand there is a lot I don't know about being an incarnated soul. The other day you said that, "During what we believe to be our awake time we are most asleep. During what we think of as our sleep time we are more awake and freely experience our divine nature".

You also said that, "Most personalities experience life through physical consciousness versus spirit consciousness." Would you please explain about both of these statements?

Anna: You have brought forth teachings and have inspired others by your ongoing education during your sleep time. We would also like to acknowledge that everyone "travels" during sleep time. Although the majority of personalities do not remember this time as clearly as you do, they do travel to other planes of consciousness while their physical form is asleep.

Most recently you have begun to change your sleep pattern. Your physical body sleeps and during this time your multifaceted being "wakes" up. Many things occur during sleep time. Your physical body goes into a state of deep relaxation. During sleep time body systems begin to communicate. Although a part of your consciousness leaves the physical body, beings of light continue to watch over it. During this time your personality is also asleep and, depending on the level of relaxation, your physical form will receive a tuneup.

We have introduced why energy adjustments are important. We believe the introduction of this concept of healing will bring forth a new level of health care for many. Energy adjustments are often performed during sleep time. During sleep time one's brain waves go into delta and theta waves. More importantly the mind also goes into a state of deep relaxation. Your mind is not a part of your physical body, however your mind does play a significant role concerning one's health both mentally and physically.

When the physical body and the mind are in states of relaxation, healing can occur. Your mind is fueled by thought energy. As you know, one's thoughts can empower or disempower one's life.

What we are suggesting here is that personalities begin to restructure the way they think of their sleep time. Doing this, we believe, will begin to shift the consciousness of those who follow our guidelines for creating a healthy shift into dreamtime.

We want to be clear here that you are an incarnated soul. Thus you are a multifaceted being. We have discussed in other discourses that incarnated souls are both spiritual and physical. Many personalities focus their consciousness on what we call body consciousness, meaning personalities focus on experiences known to them during the time they experience as being awake.

You view this time as your only reality. Personalities see themselves as flesh and blood. Clearly you are more, much more, than this. As we have said in several discourses, when the child is born the light body of the soul encircles the infant child. With each breath physical and spirit become united. For thousands of years humankind has separated the physical and spiritual aspects of self. Consciousness has been experienced with the focus in physical consciousness. We now offer this shift in consciousness of soul consciousness. Soul consciousness acknowledges that your physical body is encased in a body of light. This body of light is capable of astral travel. Soul consciousness affirms that the creative spark of God is within you. Soul consciousness does not separate experiences. Soul consciousness understands that the experiences in the astral planes of consciousness are as "real" as the experiences on the earth planes of consciousness.

Soul consciousness fully embraces the time when the physical body sleeps as a time for renewal and repair of the physical form. Soul consciousness understands that travel to the astral planes during the body's sleep and repair time is as full and rich with experiences as time during what they perceive to be awake time. Soul consciousness does not separate the experiences, but being a multifaceted incarnated soul integrates the experiences.

Katye: Anna why are the majority of personalities unaware of travel to the astral planes of consciousness?

Anna: One cannot be aware of that which is not in one's consciousness. When viewing one's experience through the physical senses one will have a limited focus of, shall we say consciousness, thus experiences. We have discussed in other discourses the infant child is born with heightened senses. The infant child has constant connection to the world of spirit. The infant child uses these heightened senses to assess the world around them. During the early months of infancy the infant does not travel to the astral planes. Anchoring one's spirit into the physical form is an ongoing process. The infant child has an ongoing connection to soul and spirit guides.

When the light body and physical form have fully merged, travel into the astral plane begins. This usually begins by the time the child is around one year old earth time. By this time the light body and physical body of the developing child have fully aligned. Parents themselves focus primarily on physical experiences, thus are unschooled in the teachings of the soul. We will teach more about helping the infant child assimilate the experiences of dreamtime with waking state in a future discourse. We will now focus on how each personality can begin to use this time of physical sleep to expand their consciousness, thus their life.

To understand one's experience in the astral planes of consciousness, one must first learn to understand dreams versus astral travel to different planes of consciousness. Dreams are one way the soul helps the incarnated being remember what has taken place on the astral planes as a part of astral travel. Some dreams are unconscious messages. They are being played out through language of the soul. These messages are symbolic. We refer to these working dreams as one way the personality gets a glimpse into their unconscious process. Dreams will bring forth fears, desires, and challenges of life. These fears are often held in one's unconscious. By paying attention to one's dreams one can begin to bring into the awakened state of consciousness areas of life that one can focus on for growth and expansion.

The majority of personalities are aware that they dream during sleep time. Many say they do not remember their dreams. This of course is because once the personality opens their eyes they become focused on physical experiences.

Astral travel is not a part of dreaming. Astral travel is simply a time during sleep state of the physical form that the incarnated soul travels through its body of light into other realms of consciousness. Consciousness is not limited to the physical experience. During astral travel the incarnated soul travels to the astral planes of consciousness.

Many personalities travel to the astral planes during sleep time to visit those who have transitioned (birthed into spirit) from the earth planes to the astral planes of experiences. Most personalities have no understanding of the ongoing experiences in the astral planes of consciousness. For this reason, most personalities process these experiences as dreams. In awakened state, with the focus on physical consciousness, the personality thinks of time spent on the astral plane as time that was not real. We tell you now that astral experiences are as real as any experience one has during awake time. We tell you the afterlife on the astral planes is as rich with experiences as the life on the earth planes of consciousness.

During astral travel the incarnated soul receives teachings, soul reviews, insights, inspiration, guidance and communications directly from their soul and counsel of light.

Katye: I know from my astral travel experiences I have brought forth the teachings of my soul. I haven't fully understood about astral travel because it was not a part of my awake consciousness, I just did it naturally. I remember about eighteen years ago a woman who came to York to give intuitive readings told a friend of mine that I was a traveler. I was very embarrassed. Now I freely embrace this aspect of my multifaceted self. Anna, you have said that, during sleep time, we are more awake and freely experience our divine nature. How can we begin to integrate this into our physical awake time?

Anna: We believe our conversations will help personalities embrace they are incarnated souls. When personalities begin to use sleep time as a time of travel for one's light body they will begin to bring more of their soul into their lives. Humankind will begin to experience multidimensional living, thus experiencing their divine natural.

Katye: How can we make this paradigm shift?

Anna: As with any paradigm shift, one must shift into a new consciousness, meaning expanding what one thinks of as reality to include a new belief. To begin to shift into soul consciousness, one begins to reconnect to one's inner guidance, which of course is soul directed and inspired. Simple changes in one's life will allow for a consciousness shift. Using time when the physical form is asleep as time for astral travel will bring forth messages from soul into one's life.

The first shift in consciousness that we suggest is, one should prepare for dreamtime consciously. In other words, begin to allow your physical body and your mind to relax about an hour before you take your body to bed. You do this by disconnecting from the experiences of the day. Turn off the television and put down any reading material which is overly stimulating. For those of you who are exhausted from the day's experiences, we would propose that you begin to reevaluate the structure of your life. This shift in consciousness will not take more time out of your busy life. We would remind you that most of the business of your awake time has been very unproductive.

Begin a practice of reflection and evaluation of your day. We would suggest families turn off the electronic appliances and communicate with each other the events of the day. Honor your experiences which you consciously created. Begin to understand the experiences which were part of an unconscious process.

With conscious awareness, begin to transition into sleep state of the physical body by sleeping in a room which has been created for this experience. You call these rooms your bedrooms. A term we now bring into your consciousness is sleep chamber. Optimal use of this sleep chamber would be used only for sleep. When this is not possible, the space should be free of clutter and without electrical appliances turned on. Having spent time preparing the mind to release the clutter and activities of the day, turn your consciousness toward slowing down the physical body. You can do this by taking a few deep breaths and consciously asking your spirit guides and soul to help you make this transition into sleep state. Your ongoing experiences during the day and your ability to shift conscious focus to dream state will determine your astral experience.

Astral experiences during dreamtime offer information and guidance which can be used for the incarnated soul.

The second shift in consciousness is, upon leaving sleep time (waking up) continue to allow soul guidance to enter your consciousness. Simply take a few minutes to write down any information you received via dreams and experiences you remember while in the astral realms. Use this information to begin to see the patterns of your life via soul communication.

As you journey through your day, do so in an awakened state of consciousness. Take responsibility for the life you have created. Embrace the adventure of being an incarnated soul. Use this gift of life to bring forth the spark of creator god who is individualized through you. Consciously create a life with joy, peace and love in every experience.

THE SEVEN EARTH PLANES OF CONSCIOUSNESS

December 8th 2013

Katye: It was with great excitement I read again this next discourse. I began to understand the importance of my work with Anna. I also knew that I was created to bring forth this information. My soul family waited patiently for me to heal and evolve so that I could focus on the remaining years I have left as an incarnated soul on the earth plane.

On December 7th, 2013 Anna began the teachings that have excited Allan and me to our core. We have never heard of these teachings and, to be honest, Allan knows a lot, being a scholar essence. We believe these teachings from Anna are given to those who are ready to build upon their experiences on the earth plane.

We introduce to you now, the teachings that the earth plane has seven planes of consciousness, with the lower number planes being the densest planes.

Anna: You and Allan continue to feel the differences on the earth planes as feeling somewhat isolated from others, including family members. This is because you are not in the same plane of consciousness. The physical form has less density in the higher the earth planes. What many think of as the new earth is simply a higher earth plane we call the 7th plane. Many incarnating souls never make it through level 3 or 4 of the earth plane during its incarnations. It was not until the shift in the time frame of 2012 that a portal was opened permanently for those incarnated on the earth plane to travel into the higher earth planes 5, 6 and 7. The higher earth planes were transitional planes experienced by those incarnated on the earth plane. Transitional planes meaning souls being higher centering experience these higher earth planes, as well as those souls beginning the transitioning back into the astral plane. Many like you and Allan are experiencing the 5, 6 and 7 level of the earth plane. Each plane has its own vibrational rate.

Plane 1: The densest plane. This earth plane is experienced by souls who want to participate in changing energy currently on Mother Earth which is extremely dense. Many souls returning to this plane do so as an opportunity to change energy they created as a young soul. Many souls choose this plane of consciousness knowing that, if the soul goals are achieved, it will quickly shift the experiences of the personality onto higher earth planes. **Plane one is mainly about basic earth issues of survival, and a separation consciousness, fear, isolation and hardship are key experiences on this plane.** Many souls will keep coming back to this earth plane of existence for over one hundred lifetimes. Please understand that the higher earth planes were not available to incarnating souls for thousands of what you call years. This is because souls wanted to have an opportunity to change the energy that they had unleashed on the earth. It was a choice. We would like you to think of the earth planes as a rite of passage, meaning as a soul grew and returned to the astral plane upon completion of a life on the earth plane, they had grown in consciousness. Each life grew from the previous one. It took many incarnations for souls to begin to understand that, returning earth to a place of love would take devotion and fortitude as incarnating souls.

We must admit, many souls decided early on that the denseness experienced on earth after incarnating souls began to stray from the created path of the soul was not a place they wanted to continue experiencing. This did not happen, as you would say, overnight. It took thousands of earth time years to create a planet where manifesting through thought and sound were no longer experienced on earth.

Plane one is mainly about basic earth issues of survival, and a separation consciousness, fear, isolation and hardship are key experiences on this plane.

Plane 2: This earth plane is also a very dense plane of consciousness. The consciousness which prevails on this earth plane of consciousness is primarily associated with survival and creating from the sense of lack and fear, versus from the consciousness of abundance and love. The personality on this plane still creates experiences through fear, isolation and hardship, but begins to understand that there are others on the planet with the same needs. This level of consciousness thrives on group experiences of like minded personalities. **Key experiences are based on** lack, fear, need for control and rigid belief systems are experienced on earth plane 2. *Conformity is a key experience on this earth plane.*

You can begin to identify personalities in plane two by their association with groups and causes. Personalities on this plane need to belong to something or someone. FEAR is the prevailing energy, as is anger and the need to be in control of those around them and life in general.

Most likely you were born into a tribe who were experiencing the 2nd plane earth of consciousness. This means you incarnated in an environment where you might have experienced lack, fear, being controlled, or grew up having to control. You also most likely grew up with rigid beliefs which were a part of the tribe. These beliefs could have been about a certain religious dogma as well as a code of behavior you were to follow.

Earth plane two of consciousness does not embrace nor encourage individuality and has no concept of the soul other than wanting to have it saved. Seeking the group who embraces the same beliefs is very important in this plane of consciousness. There is no room for growth outside of the very narrow box which has been adapted as accepted behavior of the tribe. Conformity is a key experience.

Plane 3: The density experienced on the 3rd earth plane begins to allow room for the incarnated personality to experience more of the tribal beliefs of others. This plane is experienced by souls of various levels of growth. Power struggles prevail on this earth plane. This is the plane of consciousness that many personalities determine which beliefs will prevail as they continue to evolve. Many souls experience hundreds of lives on this earth plane. The current government running America is on this plane of consciousness as well as the 2nd earth plane. As an interesting side note, your current president wanted to take this young country into the vibration of the 5th earth plane, having no conscious understanding that he is an old soul who lived on the 4th and 5th earth planes of consciousness. However, since becoming president he has been pulled back into the 2nd and 3rd planes of consciousness. We do believe he will do far greater things with his life after he is president. This is not to minimize the good he has done, however his personality was unable to hold the vibration for the many. Martin Luther King is another example of an incarnated soul who moved a country into the 4th and 5th earth plane with a shift in consciousness. This was temporary. In the era of which we speak because of the death of a beloved leader, over the next few weeks many across parts of Africa will experience being in the 4th earth plane of consciousness. Love for a leader will shift them into the 4th plane. Again as a collective mass, they will not be able to maintain the needed vibratory rate for long. The energies which prevail in North America currently are pulling much of the country into the 3rd plane of consciousness. There are pockets of civilizations all over the earth which move freely in and out of the 4th and 5th planes of consciousness.

Key pillars of understanding:

Key experiences on the 3rd earth plane are still based on lack, fear, and need for control and rigid belief systems. On this plane of consciousness, old paradigms break down. New structures begin to form for humanity.

Hope, transformation, freedom and unity begins to replace consciousness on this level. Incarnated souls begin to release the need of rigid belief structures prevailing on the planet. Doing this, they begin to move into the 4th earth plane of consciousness. Personalities on this plane begin to be willing to hear about other beliefs without the fear of their own belief systems being the only way to be. Focus on this plane of earth is still placed on survival needs based on lack.

You can begin to identify personalities on earth plane 3 by their need for power struggles and the need for control. Drama is still a key experience for those on the 3rd plane of earth. As incarnated personalities begin to move into the 4th plane of earth willingness to hear and not be threatened by new beliefs becomes a prevailing energy.

Please understand that these earth planes can be experienced in any era. We will explain more about this in a later discourse.

Plane 4: The density on this earth plane begins to soften and personalities experience oneness and unity. This 4th plane of existence becomes more than just a thought by the incarnated soul, as it evolves into one who begins to experience this earth plane of reality. Navigating this plane of consciousness can be experienced by the incarnated personality as challenging at best. Moving fully into the 4th earth plane of consciousness requires work and dedication to living a life influenced by your soul and less by your tribal vibrational signature.

The personality begins to clear and shift old paradigms and beliefs on the 4th earth plane. It is on this plane where personalities begin to move toward an actualized being. This is the plane of consciousness where the incarnated personalities choose to bring forth the vision of one's soul or choose to step back down into the density of the 3rd plane. **This is another earth plane where many incarnated souls experience hundreds of lives before they are ready to break through the limitations on the denser earth planes.** It is here in this plane where many incarnated souls struggle to move toward the lightness of the higher earth planes or be pulled back into the denseness of the 3rd level physical plane. As we have said, hundreds of incarnations are experienced between earth planes 3 and 4. The choice becomes clear from this point onward as personalities begin to embrace the journey of the soul.

Meaning, will the personality choose to integrate the goals of the soul and create growth and expansion on the physical level or be pulled back by fear into the earth plane 3? On this 4th plane, the tribal experience begins to grow into an expanded one, based on new paradigms and beliefs. Central to this plane is a rite of passage moving one forward into a state of soul consciousness. It is however still a choice of the personality. Many personalities fall back into what is known to them versus what is unknown. For those incarnated souls who choose to move forward, it can be an exciting time as well as a time of confusion as the energy of the 5th plane begins to propel the older mature soul forward. Key experiences of growth followed by life changes or challenges are experienced by those incarnated souls on the 4th plane of earth. The 4th plane of earth is a plane of intense changes, and the choice to participate in drama or not. The fourth plane of earth is a plane where one moves forward to the higher earth planes of love and oneness, or is pulled back into the fear and power struggles associated with earth plane 3.

Key pillars of understanding:

This is the earth plane where incarnated souls begin to experience and remember soul essence contact, be it consciously or unconsciously.

This is the earth plane where choices are made to begin integrating direct influences of the soul's journey.

Incarnated souls on the 4th earth plane begin to understand how to create from love, and how much energy and power EVERY thought holds within it.

Earth plane four requires commitment in understanding how every thought one focuses on more than ten seconds holds the power to create.

Incarnated souls at this level will experience a period of growth. Incarnated souls release beliefs and structures of society which no longer work for them. These growth experiences will be followed by a choice to move forward consciously by changing and expanding one's life experiences. If the incarnated soul chooses not to move forward they will be pulled back into the 3rd plane of earth where one will experience stagnation.

Earth plane four consciousnesses is a plane of conscious creating. However many personalities are pulled back and forth between the earth planes 2, 3 and 4.

You can begin to identify personalities on earth plane 4 by their willingness to shift from a consciousness of struggle and drama of the 3rd earth plane, to one of growth and expansion experienced by the incarnated soul on the 4th earth plane. There is a strength incarnated souls begin to experience in this earth plane.

Those who have shifted into a consciousness of being both creator and created begin to fully anchor and embrace that they are an incarnated soul. Soul growth and soul expansion begin to guide one's life and the incarnated personality begins to understand that they are capable of experiencing "heaven on earth."

Plane 5: As one moves into the fifth earth plane of consciousness, the incarnated soul has passed through many levels of earth plane denseness. Choices have been made to continue evolving and growing. This is often experienced by the incarnated soul as having many life changes and major shifts of consciousness. Souls experiencing this plane of earth begin to have an expanded state of consciousness. Key experiences are unity, manifestation from love versus fear, growth, teaching, transforming, and integrating the truth of oneness of all. Religion may or may not play a part in the life of the incarnated soul. Of major importance is spiritual connection. For many incarnated souls much of the soul essence contact is still occurring in sleep state. As the incarnated soul begins to find its way on the 5th plane of earth, they begin to experience more awareness of being an incarnated soul in an awakened state of consciousness even during non-sleep time. A note here, earth plane 5 is also where many incarnated souls spend time as they are transitioning back to the astral plane. People with Alzheimer's and those birthing into spirit find themselves on this earth plane as well as the 6th plane. This of course causes issues with those in authority on the lower planes of consciousness. Simply put, those on the lower earth planes have no conscious understanding of why anyone wouldn't want to be like the typical robotic human. Differences are truly not appreciated until one begins to shift on the transitional earth planes of 5 and 6.

Earth plane 5 is still a time where the incarnated soul is working on one or two core soul issues. For these incarnating souls, this is experienced as a melting away of the personality's desires. As integration continues, one begins merging of the desires of soul. Once an incarnated soul arrives on this plane of consciousness, the focus of letting go of things of the earth becomes paramount. During this transitional state, the incarnated soul begins to defer to the goal of the soul. The 5th earth plane may be experienced for fifty or so lifetimes before the incarnated soul is ready to let go of personality.

Embracing that one's life has been created for the purpose of soul growth and expansion begins on this 5th plane of consciousness. It would do you well to understand the incarnated soul still has a physical structure. This must be cleansed of the fear of merging into a unified field of oneness with one's soul.

Key pillars of understanding:

Even though the incarnating personality is experiencing life in the 5th plane of the earth, the human form still has not fully integrated the light body changes. Light body changes occur as the transitioning incarnated soul experiences growth, usually beginning on the 4th earth plane.

Those incarnated souls experiencing the 5th plane of earth begin to understand that they are both creator and creation. They fully understand the power of thought and emotions, however they easily get pulled back into the 4th earth plane.

Key pillars of understanding:

Key experiences are unity, manifestation from love versus fear, growth, teaching others about soul, transforming, and integrating the truth of oneness of all.

You can begin to identify personalities on earth plane 5 by their expanded state of consciousness. Those on the 5th earth plane begin to embrace that they are incarnated souls. These incarnated souls are very focused on growth and transformation for self and those who cross their path.

Those on earth plane 5 consciousnesses fully understand the art of allowing as well as the art of allowing others to have the experiences they want to have.

To fully live and experience life in earth planes 5, 6, and 7 requires a vibrational signature of love.

The 5th, 6th, and 7th planes are transitional planes of consciousness.

Plane 6: The incarnated soul who begins to experience the 6th earth plane has been on a long journey through the denseness of the lower planes. To stay on the 6th earth plane, an expanded state of oneness and love must be experienced at all times. Attachments to the people, places and things are not as important as the goals of one's soul. These incarnated souls have fully integrated that they are souls incarnated in a physical form.

The physical form has gone through many changes and the incarnated soul begins to focus more on how to bring forth more light into the physical vehicle. Sacred codes of light being held within the Soulstar begin to activate and the incarnating soul's energy field begins to emanate a vibration consistent with the light body. When incarnating souls experience fear of any kind they are pulled back into the 4th and 5th earth plane depending on the event or issue. The event or issue will have energy associated with it which will fuel the experience. The density of the 4th plane still has a vibration of fear, although not anything like the 1st, 2nd, and 3rd planes. The fear experienced on the 6th earth plane is often associated with the fear of the unknown, versus the fear experienced by the incarnated personality during one of its recent incarnations. This fear is deeply felt by those on the lower earth planes.

When an incarnated soul experiences being pulled back to the 3rd or 4th earth planes, it would serve them well to ask for a soul life review, as well as time with its higher counsel of wisdom. Also consulting a trusted teacher and guide who projects attributes of being on the 6th earth plane would help at this time. As the incarnating soul begins to experience moving back and forth between states of expanded consciousness, they do so consciously. When an incarnated soul moves back into the 4th and 5th planes of earth, they do so fully understanding that they must look within for guidance, and release that which has caused the fear.

There are few incarnated souls who are capable of keeping an expanded state of consciousness at all times. Therefore the 3rd and 4th plane of earth is where you will find incarnated souls living most of the time. However as these incarnated souls begin to understand that time is no more, the illusions and traps of the lower earth planes are experiences which they rarely experience and when they do they quickly understand soul work is needed.

The transitional earth planes of 5 and 6 bring an understanding that the only purpose for their existence is soul growth and soul expansion. It is on earth planes 5 and 6 where the incarnated soul begins to understand that incarnated beings on these earth planes are few in number. Time spent on the lower earth planes brings another adjustment to the evolving soul as it begins to spend more and more time on the higher earth planes. Friends and loved ones begin to experience the incarnated soul as uninterested in them and their lives. This is not the case; however without an understanding of incarnating souls being on different planes of earth at any given time, it is hard to explain the reasons behind the seemingly odd behavior.

It is for this reason that the incarnated soul on the 6th plane begins to grieve for those they feel they are leaving behind. Please understand, the incarnated souls on planes 5 and 6 will continue to associate with other incarnated souls on the lower earth planes. After all, the soul contracts are binding no matter which earth plane an incarnated soul has evolved to.

Incarnated souls understand living on the 5th and 6th planes REQUIRES an expanded state of consciousness at ALL TIMES. The trap for incarnated souls on the 5th and 6th earth planes of consciousness is, being pulled into the dramas of those they have soul contracts with who are still living on the lower earth planes.

An example we would like to give you at this time is this: in this plane of consciousness an incarnated soul practices, and begins to integrate into one's life, the art of allowing. An incarnated soul being pulled back into the 4th plane of earth must learn they are connected to the experience through their emotional resonance. The incarnated soul has not completely shifted into the art of allowing. Getting caught in the energy of those who are screaming for change of any particular situation will pull the incarnated soul into the drama.

They will experience resentment and frustration with the events which pulled them back into the 3rd and 4th planes of earth. The incarnated soul will be pulled back into the 3rd and 4th earth planes, and will stay there until they choose to move back into the 5th earth plane. This may take years depending on the attachment to the situation. Once back into the 5th plane of earth, they will begin to transform their attachment to the situation or event and the other personalities involved.

An incarnated soul on the 5th and 6th earth planes will experience the same event, but through the lens of unconditional love and nonattachment. The incarnated soul's emotional resonance has shifted into one of nonattachment. The incarnated soul on the 5th and 6th planes of earth begins to shift into the energy of transformation. Looking at the situation through nonattachment they will not be pulled back into the 4th earth plane where the density of fear still resides.

These homospiritus have direct communication with soul and are experiencing an expanded state of consciousness in all areas of their lives. The few times they get pulled back into the 3rd and 4th planes they quickly know that they have lost their center and quickly shift to the 5th plane where growth and expansion are experienced.

Key pillars of understanding:

Usually those who begin to embody 5th and 6th plane consciousness do not stay on the lower planes for long. However it is possible that an event, a new relationship and or embracing the magnificence of who you are can shift an incarnated soul back into the safety of the fourth planes of consciousness.

You can begin to identify personalities on earth plane 6 by the peace and presence they radiate, which is love in its purest sense of the word. The Dalai Lama and Thich Nhat Hanh are two such examples of incarnated souls capable of experiencing expanded states of love, thus living on the 6th plane of earth most of the time.

Plane 7: As we have previously explained, in the earth year of 2012 was a shift experienced on 4th, 5th, and 6th earth planes of consciousness. Incarnated souls began to know that a change of consciousness had occurred. Before the shift, incarnated souls on the 2nd and 3rd planes of consciousness were the ones who made the jokes about the end of the world coming. On the lower earth planes, the shift was a momentary experience that something was occurring, but the denseness of the lower planes did not allow the shift in consciousness to occur.

Many incarnated souls found themselves caught up in the excitement of the shift. When they woke up on December 22nd 2012 and experienced life on earth was basically unchanged, they shifted back into living primarily on the 3rd and 4th planes of earth. Many of these incarnated souls experienced a feeling of being disappointed because the shift did not occur. What these incarnated souls misunderstood was that the shift did occur, however it did not occur on the lower earth planes. On the 4th earth plane, the portal into the 7th plane is experienced only in dream state, and few are remembering upon this upon awakening.

Many incarnated souls who find their way into the 7th earth plane of consciousness are experiencing it as a new earth. This is understandable.

These incarnated souls have not fully realized that the 7th earth plane is a place of sound, light and conscious creating, much like it was on earth eons ago. On the 7th plane, vibrational consciousness is based on pure love and unity of one. On this level, incarnated souls still in human form begin to understand fully that they are truly a homospiritus and although they are still of physical form, they are more light form than physical matter. These incarnated souls continue to project an image of being physical matter, however their consciousness is one of love. The incarnated souls who find their way to the 7th plane of earth have not fully integrated that they are the pioneers who are co-creating a new earth.

These souls have not fully integrated that they are birthing into consciousness a new earth for those who care to participate. The 7th level earth is vibrational, and any thought which is not of love will quickly take one back into the 5th or 6th earth planes. Again, many who are experiencing the 7th earth plane do so in their dream state with little remembrance of the experience.

Katye experiences the 7th earth plane as a place her dolphin companions no longer need to limit their lives in the water. Again, this is a form of her creating.

Incarnated souls on the 7th earth plane create through thought and sound. The 7th plane of earth is not solid mass. It is liquid, and is contained by conscious thought and held within the thought is vibration.

We hope that the many discourses with Katye Anna have given you an understanding of the role that your soul plays in your life. You are indeed a grand design, created through conscious intention of your soul. Our lives on the earth planes of consciousness can take many twists and turns, however interwoven through the fabric of our lives is a soul inspired life. Even when the personality has strayed far from the desired plans of the soul, our soul continues to create ways in which we will remember the truth of our magnificence. Through astral time while sleeping, and whispers from our spirit guides, to intuitive messages, and interactions with those we have soul contracts with our lives are infused with the energy of our souls.

Choose today to be the day you claim your magnificence. Embrace that you are an incarnated soul, and within you is the spark of creator God. Let today be the day you embrace soul consciousness and begin to create your life and your world through the creative spark of your soul.

Affirm: I embrace the magnificence of who I am, a creative spark of God. Today I allow the creative spark of my soul to shine through my life.

Anna: We acknowledge that the information contained in the discourses may confuse some personalities. In actuality confusion is not a negative. From confusion springs questions and inspires action to shift one's consciousness.

As we move forward with our teachings, we will continue to build on these teachings of light. We are sure we have given our students much to process. We look forward to a time of discussion with those who care to learn more.

CHAPTER 6

SAMUEL REFLECTS
ON HIS LIFE

We now return to Samuel's life. If you remember, Samuel was born in the era of 1953. His soul chose many experiences and soul contracts with other incarnating souls which would create a world where Samuel could learn lessons of empowerment, self-love and acceptance. The year we enter Samuel's life is 2002. His life, like all of our lives, has taken him on a journey of many twists and turns. Through life choices Samuel's life has evolved. He was raised in an environment where he was not encouraged to bring forth the creative expression of his soul. He has evolved into a man who is motivated by love. As with each one of us, Samuel has on-going soul essence contact. His life is infused with stirrings of his soul, even though he is not consciously aware of this relationship.

It is the year 2002. Samuel is sitting by his mother's hospital bed listening to the respirator that is doing her breathing for her. The years had taken their toll on his beautiful mother. In 1987, his mother was diagnosed with breast cancer. She fought the long battle. She fought hard, but to no avail. Finally in the year 2002, the cancer which began in her breast now invaded her liver and lungs, and the doctors said it would be a matter of days before his mother died.

As the young nurse took care of his mother's physical needs, Samuel's mind drifted off to his life with his mother, and he began to think of his early childhood memories. By the age of two, Samuel understood that his father ruled the house. Even as a child, Samuel understood that his father expected his young son to obey the very strict code of behavior adopted by his family. His mother had tried her best to shield him from the wrath of his father, but it seemed like very early on, Samuel and his father William clashed. The soul contract made in the astral plane had been forgotten by both Samuel's mother and father. No one in Samuel's tribe remembered the way of the soul. Samuel was not given space to bring forth the creative expression of his soul.

Long before Samuel had been born his father had established the rules of the family. His father saw his young son as an inconvenience. His wife began to put her time and attention into loving her son. The tug-of-war began from the first day Samuel came home from the hospital. His father demanded his wife be the dutiful preacher wife and put the needs of God before the needs of the child.

Elizabeth tried her best to keep her promise to her young son as they left the hospital together. However, she quickly bent to the demands of her husband and put the needs of her demanding husband before her own promise to protect her son and create a world in which he would thrive.

Samuel grew up in the 1950's. Children were expected to be quiet and conform. Samuel remembered his father telling him this over and over. Being raised by his father who was a man of God was difficult for Samuel. Samuel's father had tried to instill in his young son and those he preached to that God was an unmerciful god, an unforgiving God. Anyone who did not obey the word of God would burn in hell come judgment day.

Samuel remembered being confused by his father's words, because as a very young child he knew that the one his father called God was not a punishing God. He didn't know how he knew this, but he knew his father was wrong. This of course would lay the ground work for many clashes between father and son.

Katye: Anna, even though Samuel didn't remember being an incarnated soul it seems he had some understanding of the world of spirit.

Anna: Yes, this of course was the ongoing soul connection which all infants have in those very early years of life. Of course as with most children of this era, physical consciousness would take over and Samuel would find himself fighting hard to remember his truth about God being a loving God.

As Samuel continued reflecting about his life, he remembered at a very early age trying to tell both his parents that he had special friends of light. Samuel of course did not understand that his parents had forgotten being incarnated souls, so they could not hold space for their young son who talked to his "imaginary friends". William forbid his young son to talk about his friends of light. Sitting by his mother's hospital bed, Samuel wondered if his special friends had been the imagination of a small boy, or had they been real. There were many times during his life Samuel felt supported by something other than that which was physical. Samuel had no idea that his angels chosen for him by his soul had always been with him. Even now his angelic companions were close by Samuel's side.

Samuel's attention returned to his mother because he thought he saw a flicker of light over by his mother's bed, but just as quickly as he saw it, it was gone. Because Samuel was focused on physical consciousness, he could not see the beautiful angel which hovered over his mother's bed. Nor could he see the many other light beings and those who had crossed over who were in the room. Samuel was, however, aware of the smile on his mother's face. Samuel wondered perhaps if his mother had an awareness of something he could not see. His mother still could communicate and did so, even though she could no longer breathe on her own. The times of connection were getting rare and Samuel cherished every moment with his mother.

Katye: Anna, how sad it is that Samuel cannot see the spirit guides and departed loved one which surrounded his mother's bed.

Anna: Yes, Samuel had long ago forgotten his connection to the world of spirit. Samuel, despite being raised by a man who had no eyes to see his son and no ears to hear his son, had grown into a man of great compassion and love for self and others. He was aware that his mother was at peace and, although she would have loved to have had more time with her family, her body was shutting down.

As his mother drifted back to sleep, Samuel's thoughts took him away from the hospital room once again. Samuel remembered the first time he felt different from his friends. He loved going to school and loved learning, however he never felt like he fit in with the other children. He had a friend named Steve. He was around nine years old and his best friend Steve had a crush on a girl in their class. Samuel felt funny every time he watched his friend try and get the attention of the girl and didn't like sharing his young friend with anyone, much less a girl. Samuel thought how funny it was that after all these years he could still feel the pangs of love for his first crush, which had been his friend Steve. Of course, Samuel never told anyone about his feelings for his friend. Even at the age of nine, Samuel knew there was something different about him and he knew to keep it to himself.

Samuel wondered how the death of their mother would affect his sister Karen. They had grown apart and, in truth, had never been very close. As children, his sister Karen could do no wrong in the eyes of their father. She seemed to understand how to please their father even as a young girl. Samuel's younger sister Karen had been born two years after Samuel. Samuel remembered the many times his father would put down his Bible to hold his daughter, something he never did for Samuel.

Even though Karen was younger than Samuel, he remembered the many times she tried to get him to just follow the rules their father had set forth. Samuels's father believed in using the belt when Samuel disobeyed the rules. Thinking back, Samuel never remembered his father using the belt on his sister Karen. He did remember Karen coming to his room when he was around twelve years old and had just received a beating from his father. Both children could hear their parents arguing about William's treatment toward their son. Karen pleaded with Samuel to just get along with their father. Even at the age of twelve, Samuel knew he would continue to disobey his father because, by this time, Samuel had no respect for the man he called father.

Thoughts of his friend Jimmy entered Samuel's mind, and he found himself smiling. Little did Jimmy and Samuel know it at the time, but their friendship was one which would awaken Samuel to why he was so different. Jimmy was the son of the local undertaker. Like Samuel, Jimmy had a strict code of conduct he was forced to follow and, like Samuel, Jimmy rebelled against his father. This of course made a special bond between the boys, but it wasn't really what connected them. One day when Jimmy and Samuel sneaked away to go fishing, Jimmy talked Samuel into going skinny-dipping in the pond. Thinking back on this day, Samuel smiled because it was the events of this day that Samuel realized why he had always felt so different. During the skinny-dipping, the young boys found themselves exploring. At the age of fourteen Samuel knew what he had known but didn't understand at the age of nine. Samuel knew he was different because his first crush was a boy, and his first sexual experience was with Jimmy.

After this first experience, the boys would sneak off and enjoy their afternoons of "fishing." One day Samuel waited for Jimmy to come fishing but he never came and, after that day, Jimmy wouldn't even look at Samuel at school or church. Samuel realized that Jimmy was ashamed of being different and wanted nothing to do with Samuel or "fishing."

Samuel's attention was drawn to the young nurse's aide who was seeing to the needs of his mother. This young nurse's aide reminded him of Sally. Even after all of these years, Samuel felt regret for his treatment of Sally. When Samuel turned sixteen, his parents had encouraged Samuel to form friendships with the girls at the church socials. Samuel hated these events but would go and, for his mother, pretend to enjoy the social gatherings. By this time, many of his friends had girlfriends. Even Jimmy had a girlfriend and would find himself getting married the year he turned seventeen, because his girlfriend was pregnant.

Samuel's mother encouraged him to take Sally on a date. Sally had been a friend of Samuel's since grade school, so he felt comfortable with her. Samuel's father had questioned him about why he found no interest in girls, so to please his mother and to get his father off his back, he started taking Sally to the church socials. This was one of the few times Samuel remembered his father being pleased with him. Sally was the banker's daughter and she was a catch. Unfortunately for Sally, Samuel could not play along for long, and one day Sally walked in on Samuel and his friend Harry being sexual in the basement of the church.

The look on her face and the hurt still weighed heavily on Samuel's heart. It was never his intention to hurt Sally. Somehow Sally had found it in her heart to forgive Samuel for deceiving her and using her in this way. At the young age of sixteen, Sally had learned how to forgive. Of course this did not occur right away, for Sally briefly struggled with what was wrong with her that Samuel didn't love her the way she did him. It took a few weeks and heartfelt conversations for Sally to understand that Samuel truly didn't mean to hurt her, even though he pretended to be her boyfriend. Now at least Sally understood why Samuel never wanted to make out with her. She realized this was not because she was not good enough, or pretty enough, it was because Samuel was gay. She promised to keep Samuel's secret and forgave him and found a boyfriend who wasn't gay with whom she explored her own sexuality.

Katye: Anna, Sally was the soul who agreed in the astral planes to be Samuel's girlfriend in high school. Her goal was to learn forgiveness and to embrace self-worth. I'm thrilled to learn that Sally didn't imprint being a victim or resentment. She embraced the life lesson as the gift it was, an experience to teach her about love. Anna, I'm curious what happened to Jimmy.

Anna: Through choices of his own, Jimmy married and had three children before he was twenty-five years old. He worked hard and was a good father and husband. Jimmy, however, had a secret life which caused him great shame, and the code for the AIDS virus was activated in 1983. Jimmy died in 1984 from complications from AIDS. When Jimmy first became ill, his doctors and family had no idea of his secret life; however as word of the AIDS virus began to be known to doctors, Jimmy admitted his secret life. His family was humiliated and Samuel's father, being their preacher, assured them and his flock that Jimmy would burn in hell for being gay, and that God had punished Jimmy for being with men.

Katye: How sad that Jimmy was rejected. I remember that his soul contract knew the AIDS virus might be activated, depending on how his personality integrated his experiences as a gay man.

Anna: You must remember, Jimmy rejected himself at age of fourteen. He never found peace with being gay. This is one reason the AIDS virus was activated. The shame he felt triggered the code for the disease which had been downloaded by his soul. He loved his wife and children. Everyone had a soul contract. With Jimmy's family, including his young children, they had all agreed to lessons of love, acceptance and forgiveness.

Jimmy was only thirty-one when he died, and his oldest daughter was only thirteen. She grew up to be a woman who counseled people who were gay, as well as their families. To this day she honors the man she knew as her daddy. Her memories of his death, and the lies others told her about her father, only made her more determined to fight against bigotry and hatred. She left William's church and found a strong connection to spirit and soul as she found her way in the world. Today, Jimmy's daughter has three children of her own, and has instilled in them the values of love and acceptance of others.

Her mother, however, remains bitter to this day and never remarried. She is still a member of William's church and, in fact, is a part of a hate group which sponsors protests against gays. She wears the sign of the cross proudly and continues to play the role of victim.

Katye: Wow! Everyone involved had a soul agreement to be that which they had asked one another to be, and to bring forth opportunities to embrace love. Looks like Jimmy and his wife might need a do-over.

Anna: Remember, souls do not judge. The success in bringing forth one's soul life plans for growth is understood by the love which was shared and experienced by the incarnating soul. Although Jimmy rejected his tendency to be a gay man, thus rejecting others because he did not accept himself, Jimmy was a man who loved. In this incarnation, he believed the teachings of his church and the imprinting of his tribe. The beliefs of others took him into rejection and the code for AIDS being activated. The experiences of Jimmy were greatly appreciated by his soul and there was much healing which occurred after Jimmy left the earth planes.

As for Jimmy's wife, she still has time to turn away from hate and fear toward love. Remember, many souls create over hundred lifetimes in one era until they successfully learn the lessons of love. Let's return our focus back to Samuel.

As Samuel continued reflecting on his life, he was reminded of the card he recently received from Sally. They had remained connected through the years and he was happy to know that Sally had married the boy she met after their brief dating experience, and she was happy. Sally moved away from the town with her husband and she became a correspondent for a well known news network, and to this day continues to travel around the world as a successful journalist. In her recent card, she thanked Samuel for empowering her and helping her to learn acceptance.

Samuel smiled as he looked at the young nurse taking care of his mother and he was grateful of her reminding him of Sally.

Sally and Samuel remained friends in high school and both left town shortly after graduation. Samuel joined the Air Force. Thinking back to this time in his life reminded Samuel of how the world had changed since he was eighteen. However in regards to gays, it hadn't changed as quickly as he thought it would when he was eighteen. He had joined the service for many reasons, the main one being getting away from his father and the small-mindedness of the people in the town. He was unaware at the time, but he had entered a new phase in his life where he simply exchanged one experience of imprisonment for another.

Being rather naive of the ways of the world, he knew there would be challenges being a gay man in the military, but it was 1971 after all. The world was changing and he was sure the military would one day soon accept gays openly in the military. Thinking back, Samuel still felt that old pang of fear he felt while in the Air Force. Nothing in his life had prepared him for the experiences he had early on as a young sergeant during the Vietnam War. As a young sergeant he was there at the fall of Saigon to help with evacuations.

Nothing could have prepared him, or anyone, for the fear and desperation of those trying to flee the war-savaged country. Their orders were clear who they were there to rescue. It had been twenty-seven years since the fall of Saigon but the memories of the fear and guilt for leaving so many behind continued to haunt his dreams, even now in 2002. He stayed in the Air Force sixteen years, getting out in 1987 after the death of his partner, because he could no longer hide the fact that he was gay.

He had met Kevin during boot camp. They quickly became close friends and lovers. The stress of hiding their forbidden relationship was offset by the experience of loving each other. Their tours of duty took them away from each other, but their commitment and love was strong. Kevin left the Air Force after serving four years, electing to go to college. Kevin became a lawyer and enjoyed a successful career as litigator for equal rights for minorities.

Samuel's choice to stay in the Air Force put extra stress on their relationship, but both were dedicated to their relationship so they made it work. Since there were periods of time where they could not see each other, the men had an agreement of non-monogamy. They did so knowing their relationship and commitment to one another would never be in question. Little did they know at this time that this lifestyle choice would expose them both to joy, and eventually much pain and sorrow. In 1985 Kevin became sick. There had been whispers about a gay disease spreading throughout the gay community; however there was much denial in those early days among gay men about the plague which was going to take many lives.

Thinking back on those days still brought great sadness to Samuel's heart. Kevin died in 1987 and was the main reason Samuel left the service when he did. Having to hide the fact that he was gay from his superiors was something he did because of choice. But having to hide the fact that his beloved Kevin was dying was too much to ask. He took his accumulated leave time to spend the last few months of Kevin's life with him. He became caretaker, and this in itself took a great toll on Samuel. In 1987 there was great fear and ignorance about AIDS, and even among their friends there was great fear. The loss of Kevin made Samuel rethink his choice to stay in the service. The witch-hunts which began to take place as AIDS became known to the country was the deciding factor of Samuel leaving the service. On the day he buried Kevin, Samuel made the decision to dedicate his life to breaking down the walls of ignorance which prevailed in the world regarding being gay and AIDS.

Through taking night classes and hard work, Samuel only had a few classes to take to finish his bachelor's degree after leaving the service. As a young boy Samuel's mother instilled in him the value of education. Four years after Kevin died, Samuel became a lawyer. His life became dedicated to fighting for equal rights for gays and minorities.

Samuel remembered the fear which surrounded his life back in the late 1980's; although it had been proven that AIDS was just not a gay disease, the ignorance and fear prevailed even among gays. By 1991, Samuel had lost over fifty friends and known of many more deaths from AIDS. His career as an activist and then a lawyer for gay rights and minorities took him into the trenches of another war, unlike that of Vietnam. This war was raged against those with HIV and AIDS. They were being targeted by employers, and even health care facilities, refused service to those infected with the virus. Samuel's heart still carried the wounds from the many funerals he attended. The loss of his beloved Kevin, plus the loss of countless friends, had taken its toll on Samuel.

Samuel did not activate the AIDS virus. He had lived with the uncertainty that he had also been exposed to the virus. Little did he know that his soul had never planned on him activating the AIDS virus. It was the way Samuel embraced his life lessons which was the determining factor. Kevin's soul knowingly chose to be a part of the AIDS epidemic. Samuel's soul had chosen a life path in which the AIDS epidemic would offer Samuel the opportunity to embrace empowerment, as well as stand up against bigotry, fear and hatred.

Samuel's attention was suddenly brought back into the hospital room where his mother was dying. His mother had awakened and noticed that Samuel had tears flowing down his cheek. Elizabeth thought the tears shed were for her. Little did she know that her son had been deep in thought about his life, and the tears shed were for those brave men, women and children who had died from AIDS.

As Samuel reached for his mother's hand, he realized his father had entered the room while he had been thinking about his life. William didn't spend much time in the hospital room. He was far too busy to focus on the dying, for there were many souls to save, and many battles to fight. William believed that the cancer his wife had lived with and was now dying from was because she had truly not accepted Jesus Christ into her heart. During many altar calls, William denounced the devil which was at work in his wife's body. When faith healing did not work, he told his wife many times it was because her faith was not strong enough to heal her.

Through the years, Samuel had lost contact with his father. Although he kept in touch with his mother, William refused to allow Samuel to step foot in his home since the day Samuel announced that he was gay. The strained relationship between father and son had always pulled at Elizabeth's heart. She could never understand why William seemed to resent their son from the day he was born.

When Elizabeth found out she was terminally ill she asked both William and Samuel to get along for her sake. Both agreed to do so, however everyone could feel the tension when both men were in the same room. Samuel took the opportunity to leave the hospital for a brief walk while his father was there.

As he was walking outside the hospital, he saw someone who had affected his life greatly. With a smile on his face and love in his heart, he approached his former teacher. Mr. Smith and Samuel had stayed in touch even after Samuel had graduated from high school. It was Mr. Smith who Samuel confided in that he thought he was gay. Samuel was sixteen at the time, and Mr. Smith had been his teacher and guidance counselor during his high school years. Samuel had heard others calling Mr. Smith a faggot and queer and felt that he could trust him. Although Mr. Smith never told Samuel he was gay, he did hold space for a frightened young man to share his fears about being gay. It was Mr. Smith who gave Samuel the guidance to honor his heart and to allow his inner guidance to take his life where it wanted to go.

Little did either man understand the power behind those words, because what Mr. Smith was telling Samuel was to follow his heart which, of course, were the promptings of his soul. This wisdom from Mr. Smith would become the foundation on which the young Samuel began to build his life.

Katye: Anna, Mr. Smith had a soul agreement with Samuel. I remember their souls meeting in the Halls of Records. Their souls agreed to meet and have a relationship based on love.

Anna: Yes, Katye. They had a soul contract. The bond between teacher and student grew into a relationship of father and son over the years. Mr. Smith helped Richard to embrace his power as a young man. Samuel in turn filled Mr. Smith's life with much joy.

As the two men approached each other, Walter (Mr. Smith) opened his arms to welcome Samuel. It was as if their connection told Walter to come to the hospital just at the right time to see Samuel. Samuel told Walter that he had arrived just at the right time. Of course, once again this experience was encouraged from their souls. Even though neither man understood the role their souls played in their lives, there was truly a soul connection. Their relationship was truly inspired from the promptings of their souls.

Katye: Anna, this is what you have talked about: that even if the personality has no understanding of being an incarnated soul, the soul would still have influence over the life experiences.

Anna: As we have said, through astral time while sleeping, and whispers from one's spirit guides and intuitive messages, every personality is given guidance and help from spirit.

Katye: It would seem that William was not in alignment with his soul's life plan.

Anna: Remember Katye, you are judging William based on physical experiences. William truly believed in the word of God, and felt he was the voice of God. It would do well for those of great differences to allow others to have the experiences they wish to have. Simply move away from the chosen experiences of others if they do not conform with your chosen path.

Katye: Are you saying that, even though William has rejected his own son and preached that the wrath of hell would swallow you up if you didn't follow the word, that William is a man of love?

Anna: We simply say, "Allow others to have the experiences they need to have. Soul will use it or not for soul growth and expansion." William is creating life experiences primarily on the 2nd earth plane of consciousness. His experiences are as relevant as any others, are they not? Think if William had accepted his young son and had succeeded in having Samuel embrace the life William was living. Would not Samuel have stayed with the tribe and not have grown into the man he is today?

Katye: Wow! I never thought of it like that. This gives me a new understanding of the soul agreement, "I will be that which you have asked me to be so you can be that which you need to be."

Anna: Samuel needed to be pushed out of the tribe so he could thrive and become the man who he is today. Let's return now to Samuel in 2002.

After Samuel spent time reminiscing with Walter, he felt it was time to get back to his mother. He felt a new inner strength within him. This had always been the relationship he shared with Walter. Walter was the father to him that William never wanted to be. As Samuel walked back into the hospital room, he was relieved to see his father had gone. His mother was sleeping. He looked at her with fondness and wondered if her life would have turned out differently had she had the courage to stand up to William during her life with him. He knew his mother had tried to shield him from his father's anger and rejection, however he never remembered his mother standing up for herself.

As Samuel reflected on his life, he couldn't help but think how different Kevin's care would have been in 2002. There was still much ignorance about AIDS. Now at least the medical profession knew they could not get AIDS simply by touching someone with the disease. The fear which once prevailed even in hospitals now gave way to more compassionate care. Through education, the number of AIDS related deaths had slowed down considerably. Many lessons had been learned, not only in the gay community but also throughout the world. There was still much to do with education because people were still getting diagnosed with HIV. There was work to do in regards to gay rights. Samuel knew much of the hatred and intolerance was still present in the United States as well as other countries. Having dedicated his life to helping minorities, Samuel understood the prevailing energy toward minorities.

As Samuel continued to think about his life, he thought of the many twists and turns his life had taken. After Kevin died, Samuel turned his grief into his studies and his work. He knew his mother was dealing with breast cancer during the time Kevin was dying. As he looked at his mother, he wished he could have been there for her, but he felt it was best to stay away and, truthfully, Samuel did not want to deal with the judgment and damnation from his father. He stayed in touch with his mother, but sadness filled his heart as he realized the opportunity to share his life and all he had accomplished were gone. His mother was dying, and she would never meet his partner Jason.

Samuel met Jason in 1994. Their relationship started off as friends, but they quickly found out their connection was one that would change both their lives. When Samuel met Jason, Jason was a married man and father of four children. Jason hid the fact that he was gay and had great shame about it. Jason had even gone into therapy with a group which promoted that they could cure those who were gay. The guilt, the self-disgust and fear of being found out had caused Jason to live a life of secrecy. Jason and Samuel met in the courthouse cafeteria. It was as if they had been destined to meet, because their relationship was one which empowered both men's lives.

The first few years of their relationship were challenging at best. Samuel was openly gay, having made the decision after leaving the Air Force that he would never lie or hide the fact that he was gay again. When they met, Jason was still trying to deny the truth that he was a gay man, even to himself. It was as if their finding each other was the missing link that they both needed. For Samuel, his relationship made him smile again, and slow down his life. His life was so focused on helping others that he had forgotten how to relax and just have fun. Even though Jason struggled with his inner demons, their relationship was one of love and respect for the many twists and turns their lives had taken.

With Samuel's support, Jason began to honor the longings he had suppressed for most of his life. He began to accept that he was a gay man, and no amount of therapy and wishing it to be different would make it happen. Ending his marriage and leaving his children was one of the hardest things Jason had ever had to do. At the age of forty-four, Jason was finally doing what was best for him. All his life he tried to do the right thing for everyone else. His children were still teenagers but he felt being honest was the only way. Two of his children continued to struggle with their father being gay, but his youngest son and daughter became a part of his and Samuel's life. They even joined Samuel and Jason in a march for gay rights.

Samuel thought about his life with Jason and wondered what the future years would hold for them. Both men were committed to each other and their relationship was one which empowered both men. Samuel and Jason knew it was best for Samuel to spend as much time as he could with his mother during these last days of Elizabeth's life.

Thinking about his mother brought Samuel's attention back into the room. Elizabeth was awake and was smiling.

She motioned for the pen and paper. Elizabeth barely had energy to write, but with weakened energy she scratched on the pad of paper and asked Samuel "Do you see them?" Samuel said, "See who, mother?" Elizabeth wrote, "The angels and my parents they are here with us now." Elizabeth smiled and as she drifted off to sleep, left Samuel to think about what she had been trying to tell him. Could it be possible that his mother was seeing angels and her parents who had died years earlier? His mother never knew her mother, because she had died shortly after Elizabeth was born. Samuel wondered how it could be possible that his mother could see her mother and father.

He remembered when Kevin was dying he had said many times that he saw people who were in the room. Samuel thought at the time that Kevin was hallucinating but now he wondered. Was there something more to this life than what he could see?

Having been raised by William, Samuel wanted nothing to do with religion or God. The God his father talked about was a condemning God, a cruel God who did not answer prayers. Samuel loved his mother, and he knew she had prayed for healing and did everything she could to fight the cancer, but to no avail. Here she was this woman of faith, dying of this dreadful disease. Samuel wondered if her life and her health would have been different had she found the strength to stand up for herself in regards to William. His mother had once told him of her dream to travel, but she had never been further away than one hundred miles from the place she had been born. Elizabeth loved to read, and Samuel sent her books and pictures from his travels.

Angels, and those who had died but could now be seen by his mother, did make Samuel wonder if there was a part of his life that perhaps still needed healing. He knew that Jason spoke of his connection to a loving God. God, and things of spirit, was the one area of their lives that Samuel and Jason did not agree on.

But here he was once again, watching someone he loved dying, and she was at peace just as Kevin had been in the last few days of his life. It seemed like something beyond what Samuel could comprehend was helping his mother find peace with leaving this world. For now, Samuel was only concerned that his mother die peacefully and with no pain.

The nurse who had been seeing to Elizabeth's needs motioned for Samuel to follow her out to the hall. She told Samuel his mother's vitals were getting weak, and if there was any family to call he should make the call. His sister Karen had arrived earlier and was on her way to the hospital. Samuel called his father and relayed the nurse's message. His father said nothing and Samuel could only assume that his father would come to the hospital.

Samuel went to his mother's side and took her hand. He could see she was not in pain and in fact seemed at peace. The nurse explained that his mother's heart was beginning to fail and her blood pressure was getting weaker. Samuel asked the nurse not to remove his mother from the respirator until his sister arrived. For a brief moment, Samuel felt anger toward his father. He was once again missing, just as he had been when Samuel was born and throughout most of his life. His mother squeezed his hand just at that moment, and Samuel wondered, did this connection they shared continue even now as his mother was dying? It felt that his mother was trying even now as she was dying to do what she could not do in life: protect him from his father.

Elizabeth had always told Samuel that his father was a good man. He just was guided by God, and his faith, to save people from the perils of hell. A part of Elizabeth admired her husband for his strong faith and it was that which she loved when they first met at the age of fifteen. William had been the only boy she ever dated and the only man she had ever known as lover. Their earlier life together had been good and they worked side by side, both wanting to help others come to know God as they did. It wasn't until after Samuel was born that their lives changed.

Elizabeth loved her son even before he was born. The bond between them had been grown during her pregnancy, and she knew she would love her child. She didn't know at the time that William would feel jealous of their child and resent the baby for taking her time away from William and the work of the church.

Samuel never got to know the side of his father that Elizabeth and so many others, including his sister Karen, knew. He wondered how his life would have been different had he and his father bonded. Maybe someday he and his father would find a way to honor each other's lives. For now, Samuel only knew his father wasn't here, and he was the one alone by his mother's bedside as his mother's beautiful heart stopped beating.

For one brief moment as his own heart felt the first pangs of grief, Samuel thought he saw several forms of light. He thought someone had entered the room and touched his shoulder, but he was alone. As he looked at his mother's lifeless body, he wondered what his life would be without the presence of his mother in his life. Even though he had moved away, he had stayed in touch with his mother and had shared his life with her as much as he could.

The nurse told Samuel he could sit by his mother's side as long as he needed to. He did so until his sister and her family arrived. Karen was too late to say her final goodbyes, but Samuel assured his sister that their mother had died in peace. Samuel shared with his sister what their mother had written about seeing angels and her parents who had died years earlier. He held onto the piece of paper where she had written her last words. Samuel told his sister he would not be staying in town for their mother's funeral but would gather with a few friends to honor his mother's life. Karen tried to persuade Samuel to stay but he knew he did not want to deal with his father and the members of his church during this time of grief.

Samuel kissed his mother's forehead and knew deep within him that his mother was no longer there. This thing called death had taken far too many people Samuel loved, and he wondered why, why did he have to lose so many friends, loved ones and now his mother by the age of forty-nine. This thing called death had played a major role in his life since he joined the service.

His heart was heavy as he left the hospital, and he didn't know what to do, but there they were, his partner Jason and his mentor and friend Walter (Mr. Smith). Surrounded by his life partner and Walter, Samuel could now allow the tears to flow. He cried, deep sobbing gut wrenching tears, and he realized that this wave of emotion pouring through him was more than about the loss of his mother. Samuel was crying for all those he had lost during his life. He cried for those he could not save during the fall of Saigon. He cried for the loss of Kevin, his first true love. He cried for those who died of AIDS, and he realized he cried for his father, a man who he never understood and who never understood him.

Katye: Once again I am aware of the spirit guides surrounding all those involved with Elizabeth. Everyone is so focused on the physical experience they do not see the world of spirit.

Anna: Yes. Samuel was unaware, as most personalities are, of the role spirit plays in their lives. Samuel had felt the touch on his shoulder at the time of his mother's death. He had long ago stopped seeing his angels, so he was unaware that it was his angel letting him know he was not alone. Samuel had also seen several forms of light beings but again, having forgotten his connection to soul and the world of spirit, he pushed these visions aside. His mother had indeed been surrounded by angels and departed loved ones as her spirit, the spark of creator God, left the physical form upon the death of her physical body. And just as her soul had surrounded the physical body of Elizabeth at the time of her birth, her body of light began its journey back to the astral plane. Yes, Samuel's beloved mother had died a physical death, but her spirit, her soul essence would continue in the astral plane of consciousness.

As Samuel walked away from the hospital, he thought he caught a glimpse of his father. He wanted to go and reach out to him but he could not. In his grief, Samuel knew he did not have the strength to be rejected by his father one more time.

CHAPTER 7

ELIZABETH MOVES INTO THE AFTERLIFE

Katye: Anna, I feel so much sadness for Elizabeth and Samuel. I have so many questions, but I know it's important to share the experience as seen through the eyes of Elizabeth.

Anna: Yes, our desire is to help those who read our words begin to understand that, through every experience, each personality experiences what is needed for their own soul growth and expansion. As you have seen through the eyes of Samuel, we would like to share the process Elizabeth experienced as she left the physical form and her soul essence returned to the astral planes. As we have said in several discourses there is more, so much more than being born, living a life and dying.

As Samuel and those who loved Elizabeth were going through their own process during the final weeks and days before Elizabeth transitioned, she was also going through her own process.

Although her physical body was shutting down, her spiritual bodies were strong. In the final months and days before her transition Elizabeth began turning her consciousness toward leaving those she loved on the earth.

While her physical body began shutting down, Elizabeth was experiencing more time in the astral planes. Her times awake were few and far between as Elizabeth's soul and angels began helping her understand that her time was soon over on the physical plane of consciousness. Her dreamtime was filled with her soul and angels helping Elizabeth begin the process of letting go of physical consciousness. Her sight slowly began changing to spirit consciousness, and she began seeing through her spiritual eyes even when awake.

Elizabeth tried to communicate with her visitors, but with the breathing tube it became very hard. She was concerned, as she had always been, about her family and how her death would affect each one of them. As the time of her physical death grew closer, she tried to tell Samuel not to worry because she knew she was going to heaven. Her faith in Jesus was strong, but the closer she came to birthing into spirit, she began to have a remembrance of a spiritual nature. She herself did not understand this spiritual connection, but she knew deep within her that all was well with her soul.

She had tried to wake up enough to tell William that he would be okay without her but she was unable to gather enough energy during his last visit. Even in her deep fog she could feel his grief and she heard him whisper in her ear that someday they would walk in the garden of Jesus together. Until that time, he would continue their fight to bring sinners to know the cross. She tried to bring herself out of the haze she was in to tell him that there were angels watching over him, but she could not. She could feel the pull of something beautiful pulling her toward a beautiful light. She wanted to go toward the light, but she also wanted to stay with those she loved. Elizabeth wanted to reach out for William as he had left the room but the light was calling her home. It seemed as soon as William left the room Samuel returned by her bedside.

Oh, her beloved son! How difficult his journey has been. And now he sat by her bedside trying to console her. Telling her he will miss her and she's been a good mom. She could hear Samuel telling her to hang on, that Karen and her family would soon be there, but the brilliant light was becoming brighter. Try as she did, the light began to engulf her and she could feel herself leaving her physical form.

She felt very light as she began to be pulled by a strange current. This current pulled her deeper into a beautiful tunnel, and it was there she began hearing beautiful music and seeing beautiful colors. Suddenly she found herself surrounded by her family and friends, but how could this be, because they had all died. In her daze, Elizabeth knew she was home, but felt a current pulling back into the room where Samuel sat next to her bed. She tried to comfort Samuel but he could not see her. His sight was focused on physical consciousness and he could not see the angels all around the room. Samuel was focused on her physical body, which lie there lifeless. It was odd seeing her physical body so still, so lifeless while here she was in this new body of light.

Elizabeth tried to console her daughter Karen when she walked into the hospital room to discover that she had arrived too late. Her mother had died before she could tell her one last time she loved her. Elizabeth reached for her daughter but to no avail. Like everyone around her, Karen was focused on her lifeless physical body. Elizabeth could only watch as those she loved began the process of grief. Samuel told his sister he would not be attending the funeral, and he would contact her in a few days.

Shortly after Samuel left, William entered the room. Again, Elizabeth tried to get him to see that, although her physical body was dead, she was still with him. Of course like all the rest of those in the room, William was only concerned that his wife had died. He kissed his wife's lips one last time and Elizabeth could sense how lost he was already feeling without her. No one really knew this man she had loved for fifty-four years. His love of Jesus was one of the reasons she had fallen in love with him as a young teenager. They had met at a Christian youth rally. Even though William was a few years older than Elizabeth he took her faith seriously. They soon became committed to standing together to help others find their way to the cross, as both of them had done since childhood.

When she met William, the loneliness which had been such a part of her life seemed to fade away. Her first memories of childhood were of her stern father reminding her that her behavior at all times was a reflection on him. Being an only child and a daughter, she always knew she was a disappointment to her father. Meeting William at the age of fifteen, it seemed her life had purpose. Her world from that day on revolved around William and their joint love of Jesus Christ. Now in this hospital room, their physical life was over and Elizabeth had no way of comforting her husband or those she loved. Elizabeth watched as William sat by her bed after sending everyone home. It was as if he was trying to prevent what was to come, life alone without his beloved wife.

Finally William made himself leave the body of his wife, for he felt he had held everyone up long enough. He watched as they placed her lifeless body on the gurney which would take her body to the hospital morgue. With a deep breath, William left the hospital room. For a brief moment, he wondered where Samuel was. Although William and Samuel never saw eye to eye, William knew his son loved his mother. William wondered how Samuel would get through the hard times ahead without Elizabeth. William knew his son had rejected the church many years ago, as he had rejected his father.

As William left the hospital room, Elizabeth wanted to follow him but, once again, she found herself being pulled into the beautiful light. She knew that William and those she loved were being watched over by their spirit guides, even though they had no understanding of them.

Feeling the pull of energy pulling Elizabeth into the beautiful tunnel made her think about her dreams and going through this same beautiful tunnel while her physical body had been sleeping. She had no memories of this when she was alive. Elizabeth slowly became clearer about what just happened on the earth planes of consciousness. She had died. Her body and her personality were no more. For a brief moment Elizabeth felt a pang of remorse for experiences she had while on earth. As Elizabeth's light body moved into the astral realm of consciousness she realized, although life on earth had ceased, her soul essence was still a part of her light body. Her light body continued consciousness in the astral planes of consciousness.

As she began to reorient herself to the astral planes of consciousness, she realized she was in what was known to her as heaven. Elizabeth looked around and she could see other light bodies. Her mother and father who had both died years earlier were here to help reorient her to life in the astral planes of consciousness. How strange it was that Elizabeth never knew her mother, but here in this place she felt like she had known her forever.

Elizabeth was amazed how different her light body felt from the physical form she had experienced during her earthly incarnation as Elizabeth. Elizabeth realized she was still very connected to her family. It was as if she still had a connection with them, although they were all unaware of this. Now more than ever before, she felt love for those she had left behind on the earth planes of consciousness.

Elizabeth knew it was soon time for her life review, and she couldn't help but think of her family she left on earth. Elizabeth moved her consciousness toward the council of wisdom and those who had gathered in the Hall of Records to view Elizabeth's life. She understood this life review was for her soul, to understand which parts of the sacred and binding soul contract had been fulfilled during her incarnation.

She watched as the council of wisdom brought forth her sacred soul contract, its seal intact since the day her soul agreed to the contents contained within the sacred document. It was with excitement and some uneasiness that she watched them break the seal. She began remembering now the plans her soul had for her incarnation. Her soul had chosen acceptance as its goal, and had been born in the era of 1933. She incarnated when fear on earth was high during the great depression. She was born into the family of Sara and Edward, who agreed to teach her about empowerment. They agreed to raise her in an environment where faith as a Christian was very important. Her soul had chosen the goal of acceptance, knowing that this would allow opportunities for its personality to experience rejection. Elizabeth's soul had chosen to experience having her young mother die shortly after childbirth, leaving her with a father who resented his young daughter for taking his love away from him.

Her soul chose such an experience because it knew the opportunity this would give for soul growth. Elizabeth understood now as she had not during her life on earth, that it was never her fault that her mother died when she was born. Of course Elizabeth had forgotten any concept of soul, much less soul contracts for soul growth, and her personality had imprinted guilt and shame.

Her father never got over his grief, and took every chance he could to remind Elizabeth that she took his wife from him. Living in the country, her father worked hard on the multifamily owned farm, and had little time or energy for his daughter. There was always an aunt or a hired baby-sitter to see to her physical needs. Being born during the depression Elizabeth learned early on that life was hard. Church was a huge part of their lives, and it was there the young Elizabeth learned about love. Love of Jesus.

She began to understand how many choices and experiences were fueled by the contracts of her soul. Elizabeth's soul had even chosen Christianity as a part of its life's plan. She realized her soul had carefully chosen other souls such as William and Samuel. Their souls had chosen Christianity to play a major role in shaping the environment which would open the doorway for many growth opportunities. Her love of Jesus and her faith was the foundation for her life, and was the connecting energy between her and William.

As the council of wisdom continued to show Elizabeth defining moments in her life, she watched the viewing screen and saw the day her father introduced her to the woman who he was going to marry. At the age of eight, Elizabeth had hoped that this woman, named Betty, would grow to love her. Sadly, that was not the case. Elizabeth remembered feeling even more lonely as her father and Betty had children of their own. By the age of eleven, Elizabeth was responsible for taking care of her sister and brother while Betty helped her father with tending to the many needs of the farm.

Church was her only outlet. Elizabeth couldn't wait until Sunday came, because this was the one day her father had some time to spend with the family. They would spend the entire day at revival meetings. Her grandfather and father were elders in the church, and Elizabeth loved watching them as they did the Lord's work.

She watched the viewing screen and remembered the dreadful day when she was told at the age of fourteen that her father had been killed in a farming accident. After that day, Elizabeth turned to her faith even more for solace. She lived for going to revival meetings, for it was there she could find peace.

It was at one of these revival meetings she met William. Watching her life unfold she now understood that William's soul and her soul had agreed to meet and build a life together. Their love of Jesus connected them. It was also what created a strain on their marriage, especially after Samuel was born. They were married when Elizabeth was only seventeen. She had Samuel before she turned nineteen. Having no mother to raise her, Elizabeth vowed to herself that her child would always know he/she was loved by her. Little did she know that the child she loved so much would affect William in very different ways.

Watching the viewing screen of her life, Elizabeth was shown the day she gave birth to Samuel and the promise she made to him as they left the hospital. Sadly, it was a vow she did not keep, and again Elizabeth had imprinted shame and remorse for not doing more to help the son that she loved and the man that she loved, love each other. William hadn't even been there when Samuel was born. He wasn't there when mother and child came home from the hospital. Watching her life as it unfolded, each choice she made along the way made her understand how her soul had planned her life.

She understood how the code for her breast cancer was released because of her emotional health. She was shown the many times and the many ways she put the needs of others before her own. She watched as her need to nurture those around her stemmed from her own need to have someone nurture her. Her choices to put others first were also ingrained in her through the teachings of her church. Self sacrifice and putting others first were what women did, even the scripture supported this belief. By the time she discovered the lump in her breast the cancer had metastasized into her lymph glands. The year was 1987. She was fifty-four years old.

Elizabeth watched the screen as it showed the day she told William about her cancer. She watched as he told her to get on own knees and asked God's forgiveness. Their faith taught that God would heal if the heart was pure.

What Elizabeth did not know until her life review was how William fell to his own knees when he was alone and asked the Lord to spare his wife from the torture he watched others go through as their pastor.

Telling her children was also hard, and she tried her best to shield them from the truth of how frightened she was. Both Karen and Samuel offered to come home immediately but she told them she had wonderful support from the church and William. As Elizabeth watched the screen, she saw how, once again, she put taking care of others before her own needs. Truth was, at the time, she would have loved to have seen both her children. She knew they had busy lives and in truth she didn't have the energy to cope with the stress of William and Samuel.

She could clearly see by the past life review how she never fully embraced self-love, nor did she ever allow anyone to take care of her. After her first mastectomy, she felt as if everyone could see that she had been punished for not serving the Lord. As she viewed the screen she could see she had worked hard and tried her best to be a dutiful wife to William, but no matter how hard she tried she never felt that she was enough.

Watching the screen, she saw many choices and many lives she had touched in positive ways during her life. She had no idea of the lives she had helped simply by taking a meal to a family in need at just the right time or offering a ride to someone who needed to go to the doctor. As she watched her life unfold, she could clearly see a woman who worked hard, loved Jesus, and was devoted to her family and friends. Here in this place of love, she understood what she had not comprehended during her life: that her love of Jesus had become distorted, and her belief in hell and condemning people as sinners were part of her life lessons. Her soul had chosen Christianity as a path because it wanted to use the chosen religion as the foundation for its life.

Her soul also chose Christianity and with it, the goal of acceptance, because a soul goal was to accept other paths and other's choices. Elizabeth had not accomplished this soul goal. Instead she used her faith to judge others, and participated in events and beliefs that caused others pain. Yes, she was motivated by love and the word of God, but here in the astral planes of creation she understood that the only true path was a path of love and no judgment of self and others.

She watched as her life unfolded, and she could see that the theme of her life had been love, love for others. Although she had lived a life of devotion to others, she never understood how to let others love her back. She understood now that the cancer wasn't a punishment, but was planned by her soul as a means for soul growth. Elizabeth realized her cancer had been downloaded by her soul and it was Elizabeth's life choices which turned the key for the disease on.

She realized her soul had planned many of the relationships with other souls prior to her birth. Having the goal of acceptance, Elizabeth had struggled from her earliest memories. She had felt rejected by her father and even her mother, although she had died soon after she had been born.

Of course Elizabeth, as most personalities, had not remembered having a soul or having soul contracts, so she imprinted that something was wrong with her that those she loved left her. Even her children left home as soon as they could and, although she had told them she understood, she carried an ache in her heart. Elizabeth always knew in her heart that Samuel would leave home as soon as he could, but she thought Karen would stay close by her father's side. Now, viewing her life, she realized that both children had dreams and plans of their own, and in truth both children had to leave home in order to thrive.

The council of wisdom helped Elizabeth to understand the lives she had changed, and the good she had done while on earth. They also helped her understand that the cancer which eventually took her life was not a punishment by God or her soul. This was simply the path her life took because her personality had never embraced self-love and putting her own emotional needs first.

Her soul had chosen other souls who would offer her life lessons of self-love. She could clearly see that both her children had learned how to love themselves, as well as grew up to be adults which empowered others through their lifework. Elizabeth had always worried that Samuel would not find his way into the kingdom of God, but now clearly understood this was because of the beliefs of her church, and had nothing in truth to do with love. She understood now that Christianity was the path her soul had chosen for its soul growth, but was only one path. She had believed that those who were non-Christian and had not been baptized in the name of the Lord would find themselves burning in hell come judgment day. During her life review, Elizabeth could clearly see she believed she was acting in love. Her beliefs had been adopted from her family and the church. These beliefs had determined the path she would take during her life. She realized she never questioned her faith, why would she? She knew that Jesus was the only path to everlasting life. Elizabeth understood now that she had lived her life rather unconscious of there being any other way.

She realized that her children had tried to show her another way but she rejected any path other than the one she had been taught as a child. During her life review Elizabeth saw that this was a pattern her soul had done in many recurring lives.

Now that her physical body had died the essence of who she was during her life was still experiencing consciousness in a different form. Her connection to those she loved was on-going as were many of her soul contracts.

Elizabeth understood that her essence would someday fully recombine with her soul but for now she would begin to create her little piece of heaven here on the astral planes of creating.

Elizabeth was excited as she knew those she loved who were still living on the earth planes would find their way to her little piece of heaven during sleep time. She felt saddened by the knowledge that her loved ones were grieving and might continue to because they had no concept of the afterlife as she herself did not during her life.

Elizabeth wondered how she could have forgotten this place of love here in the astral planes of consciousness. She knew there would be opportunities to grow as well as still help her loved ones, but she also understood that she would have time to learn many of the life lessons she had not learned while on earth. She began this new journey of choosing not to view or go back to earth during her funeral.

She knew her loved ones would not know she was there, and she also knew their angels would be with those she loved. For now she would focus on creating her little part of heaven. As she thought about what to do first she thought of the mother she never knew during her life on earth. As quickly as she thought of her mother there she was, standing in front of a door to a beautiful home. The door was opened and, as Elizabeth watched with amazement, one by one those she knew while on earth that had birthed into spirit starting walking through the door to welcome Elizabeth. It was a grand reunion of souls who now welcomed her to her new home in the astral planes of creation.

Heaven, Elizabeth had found her way to heaven. Here she would continue to grow and evolve for soul growth. She would put the focus on her own growth and allow those she loved on the earth planes to find their way here to this place she called heaven. She had learned a lot about why she made many of her choices and understood that there was still time to learn about self love here on the astral planes of consciousness. Though she no longer had a physical body she still had consciousness and, through her light body, she would continue to connect with those with which she still had on-going soul contracts.

She knew what she had forgotten while on earth, that those she loved, as well as every sentient being, had their own path to live. She would reconnect with her loved ones here in her own little piece of heaven. She knew that she could connect at any time with her loved ones still on earth. She also understood that if they felt her presence too soon, with no understanding of the afterlife, that feeling her presence could cause those she loved more grief.

For now Elisabeth turned her consciousness toward thoughts of loving herself and relaxing in the truth that, on the astral planes of creation, one was always in the eternal present moment.

CHAPTER 8

I WILL BE THAT WHICH YOU NEED ME TO BE

The year was 2014. It had been twelve years since the day Samuel left the hospital after the death of his mother. Now here he was again, on his way to the same hospital where his father was dying. As the plane he was on flew him back to the town he once called home, Samuel thought about his life since the death of his mother.

Something had happened to Samuel on that day in the hospital parking lot where he cried in the arms of his beloved partner Jason and his mentor and adopted father Walter. Samuel had not realized how much grief he had carried with him, and how losing so many friends to AIDS had caused him to focus on the hardships of life. He had continued his life's work, fighting for the rights of minorities and especially gay rights. With the help of Jason he began to enjoy life and he found himself learning about spirituality. Samuel had realized how void his life had been after rejecting the church and those in it. He also realized that he had become as judgmental toward the ways of his father, and those who believed in Jesus as savior as his father and his supporters had been toward him and others who did not profess Jesus as savior.

Through spirituality, Samuel had found a path that allowed for the existence of a God of love. He left the doctrines of the church, but formed a love relationship with the man called Jesus. He embraced the universal path of love. He wondered if he could use what he had learned about love to forgive his father.

They had kept in touch mainly through his sister Karen since the death of their mother. Samuel had only been back to his childhood town a few times since the death of his mother. Once was to pay tribute to Walter. That visit home also was the turning point in his relationship or lack thereof with his father.

Walter retired from teaching in 2004. Because of his work and tireless dedication with at risk students and youths, he was honored in a special ceremony. Samuel recalled the look on Walter's face as hundreds of students and those whose lives he had touched gathered to celebrate his work and his life.

While Samuel was home for the event, he went to visit the cemetery where his mother's body had been laid to rest. He was surprised to see his father had chosen such a lavish tombstone, for his father was never one to waste money.

What Samuel didn't know, was William had continued to visit the grave of his wife weekly, taking flowers to the grave. Nor did Samuel know of the toll his mother's dying had taken on his father. He had gone to see his father in 2004 when he was home to honor Walter. He had had a dream, and felt that somehow his mother was encouraging him to reach out to his father. Knocking on the door of the home he had been raised in was one of the hardest things Samuel had ever experienced. He wasn't sure if his father would let him in the house, but he did. Samuel was surprised to see what his sister Karen had told him. His father, once a man of stature, now seemed old and defeated.

Of course Samuel had no way of knowing that the death of his mother also had changed his father. His father, being a man of God, had prayed unceasingly since the day Elizabeth had told him of her cancer.

He believed in a merciful God as well as a condemning God. William had dedicated his life to God and questioned why God was taking his Elizabeth from him. William knew Samuel blamed him for the stress their relationship had caused Elizabeth, and he knew his son did not understand why he was not with his wife when she died.

He wasn't there because he had been praying for one last miracle that would spare his wife. When receiving the call that his wife was really dying, William felt something break within his heart. After her death, he continued to preach the Word of God, but something had changed deep within him. William had dreams of his Elizabeth being in heaven. There were many times he swore he could smell her perfume after he woke from a dream. Of course he pushed the dreams and thoughts of his wife aside, for he had no remembrance of the afterlife. Little did William know that the dreams were real. He had visited his wife in her little piece of heaven. It was in a dream that he saw Samuel knock on his door and it was because of his ongoing love for Elizabeth that he opened the door. William had read in the papers about the dedication ceremony for Mr. Smith. He knew this man had been a mentor to Samuel. He was sure Samuel would come to town for the event.

When he heard the knock on his door, it was as if he could feel Elizabeth's presence encouraging him to open the door. There was his son, a grown man, standing before him.

William remembered the first time he had laid eyes on his son. It was fifty-one years ago and William hadn't been there to take Elizabeth to the hospital. He had been with one of the elders of the church who was dying. He felt at the time that Elizabeth was surrounded by capable doctors and nurses and he knew her parents could reach him if he was needed. When he finally got to the hospital, Samuel had been born and was asleep in the hospital nursery. As he looked at his sleeping son through the glass, he dedicated his son's life to the glory of God and said a prayer of thanksgiving that both his son and his wife had made it through delivery.

Now standing here fifty-one years later, William wondered why his son and he always seemed at odds. From the time Samuel could speak, he seemed to defy William every chance he could. It's true, he hadn't been prepared for the changes in his wife after she became a mother. Once Elizabeth became a mother, she didn't put her duties to the church first as William felt she should have. William had no way of knowing that each one of them was being influenced by the life plans their souls made before incarnating.

Samuel was surprised his father welcomed him into the house. As he looked around he was surprised to see that William hadn't changed much around the house. His mother's apron was still hanging where it always hung. It had been twelve years since his mother died, but his father seemed to have aged twenty. His sister Karen was right. His father was still grieving the death of Elizabeth.

As father and son sat down together, they could not see the presence of Elizabeth. On some level she was sure they could feel her presence. Both her husband and son had found their way to heaven during their dreams. Of course both men thought it was only a dream. In truth they had found their way to the astral planes during their sleep time. It was here in this place known to them as heaven that they spent time with her. She knew neither of them understood that it was more than a dream. She was glad to see that her husband and son were together on the earth planes of consciousness, if only for a brief time. Elizabeth was aware the toll her death had taken on William. She was also aware that Samuel used her death as a defining moment in his life to change and experience more joy. Her son understood that life was too short, and he needed to embrace every opportunity as the gift it was.

As Elizabeth watched her husband and son talk about nothing of value, she was pleased that they seemed to try to respect each other for the life they had each chosen. Perhaps for the first time in their lives they were trying to listen to what the other one had to say.

Samuel didn't stay long, but this meeting between father and son would have a profound change in both their lives. They had kept in touch mainly through Karen, however both men seemed to honor the many differences their life choices had taken them on. Samuel knew his father still prayed for his soul. Samuel continued to hope that someday his father would see the error of his way, and understand that God was a loving God and hell was simply not a place at all. Samuel believed hell was an experience one could have even while living. To Samuel hell was feeling disconnected and separated from God.

Samuel took a deep breath as his plane landed, bringing him back to current time. He was happy that Walter was meeting him at the airport. They would have time to talk before he went to see his father.

Karen had texted Samuel that their father was in and out of consciousness and he was calling out for their mother. When Samuel entered the hospital room and looked at his father he was unsure what to do but his father raised his weakened hand as if motioning for Samuel to take it. As Samuel sat down by his father's bed, he realized he had never told his father that he and Jason had married last year in California. He had worked hard to help change the laws of discrimination towards gays being allowed to marry. He wondered would his father even in his weakened state notice his wedding ring.

As Samuel took his father's hand, he felt a wave of emotion hit him for which he was unprepared. His father was dying, and they would never get the chance to have a do-over. Samuel had realized his father truly loved the Lord and was a man of conviction. He realized during the twelve years since his mother's death that, although his father never understood him, he was like his father in regards to standing up for his beliefs. Both men were strong advocates for their beliefs.

Through his weakened voice Samuel heard his father say, "Do you see her"? Samuel saw no one because they were alone, or so he thought they were. In his grief, Samuel was focused on physical consciousness. The experience with his mother, at the time of her death, had helped him remember that there was more to life than what he understood, much more in fact.

So when his father asked him if he saw her, he was sure his father was talking about his mother. Samuel encouraged his father to go with his mother. He told his father to go into the light, and let Jesus and Elizabeth take him home to heaven. Although Samuel now had some concept of an afterlife, he knew his father still believed that someday he would be born again. Through his tears Samuel, his sister Karen and her children encouraged William to rest. But William continued to say, "She is here, they all are." Samuel believed at that moment that his father was somehow seeing his mother. He felt his heart opening to both his parents, who he knew had loved him the best they knew how to love him.

He held his father's hand tightly as he watched him labor for breath. He felt the tears flow for this man he never fully understood, but in the end had grown to love. As he watched his father take his last breaths, he felt a sense of peace knowing that someday they would all meet again. Samuel believed they would understand that they had each been what the other one had needed him to be.

Samuel and William had come full circle in the journey of life, one which was created by their souls. And somehow through the many twists and turns of life they had found a way to accept the chosen path of the other. Father and son had been exactly what the other one needed for soul growth and soul expansion.

Those in the room could not see that William was, once again, reunited with his Elizabeth. He was going home. William took one last look back as his son and daughter. He had loved them at best he could. He could see the angels surrounding his children. He was ready to go home to the astral planes. He would learn from the experiences he had on the earth planes of consciousness. For now he could only focus on the light and his beloved Elizabeth. As he looked forward into the light he was ready to create his own little piece of heaven, one that would include his beloved Elizabeth.

AUTHORS MESSAGE

Writing "Conscious Construction of the Soul" has been life changing for me. Embracing my soul and the plan my soul has for me has brought forth my work with Anna. I understand now that the life plan my soul has for this incarnation is a grand plan; this is also true for everyone. Understanding that our souls seek to create only love offers each one of us the opportunity to make choices that will bring forth more love on earth. I believe as we each embrace the magnificence of our souls we can return the earth planes of consciousness to a place of love.

Telling Samuel's story from his soul creating his life on the astral planes and reading how it unfolded was humbling for me. You might be wondering if Samuel is real. The answer is yes. Although we have never met in the physical he is a part of my soul family. I share his story as I will share others in future volumes of Conscious Construction of the Soul.

Anna has introduced many new ideas and concepts. We invite you to start a study group using the discourses. Anna loves questions, feel free to contact us or to join us on social media. As we travel throughout the world we look forward to meeting many of you.

Blessings, Katye Anna

Information:
To learn more about Katye Anna go to: *http://katyeanna.com*

Join Katye Anna on Facebook at: *https://www.facebook.com/ groups/Intothelightofheaven/*

Katye Anna's Blog: *http://katyeanna.wordpress.com/*

Katye Anna has also published "Into the Light." Many people think "Into the Light" is a book about dying. In truth it is a book, about living. The journeys of the people in the book share how much living and teaching they did while birthing into spirit.

The stories teach about courage and love as each person went through their own process while birthing into spirit.

Birthing into spirit isn't some catchy phrase used for the book.

Birthing into spirit is what each one of us does when our physical journey ends. Yes, there is death, but only the death of the physical. The peace and anticipation experienced by those birthing into spirit as they begin to understand that they are going "home" is real. Yes, they experience sadness about leaving the world of physical and loved ones. However, as they journey back and forth between worlds they find the pull of spirit begins to cover them with grace.

"Into the Light" offers insight that will awaken you to a new understanding of the dying process and give you tools to help those you love birth into spirit.

Our print book of "Into the Light" can be purchased at: *http://www.amazon.com/Into-Light-Lessons-Living-Taught/dp/0985140771*

About Katye Anna

Katye Anna embraces a soul inspired life. She encourages and motivates others to embrace the magnificence of who they are; incarnated souls on a journey of transformation. Katye Anna is co-founder and co-director of Pennsylvania School of Spiritual Healing. She has taught energy healing and soul transformation for twenty years.

Katye Anna is known as the dream writer. She writes her books in a semi state of sleep. This allows Katye Anna to bring forth the information from "Anna."

"Anna" has described themselves as a group of souls who no longer experience consciousness on earth. Anna is dedicated to teaching humans how to live empowered lives fueled by the wisdom and energy of their souls.

Many people have asked Katye if she is channeling Anna. Katye has never used this term because Anna is a part of her consciousness and the information flows into Katye as a steady stream of higher light consciousness.

People use many words to describe Katye Anna among them medium, psychic and intuitive. These words describe Katye Anna however they are simply words that convey someone who connects with the world of spirit. Katye Anna calls herself a traveler. She has learned how to shift her consciousness between planes of consciousness, thus she connects with souls, angels, guides and those who have birthed into spirit. Katye Anna hopes to inspire those who read her books to embrace that shifting consciousness is something we all do when we are asleep.

"Anna" shares information and insights that will inspire and challenge many who hear and read her words. They seek to help humans understand how to expand their consciousness from a physical consciousness to a spiritual consciousness.

If you have enjoyed this book, we would appreciate it if you would post a positive review. Positive reviews help us reach more people. To post a review, all you need to do is go to the review section of this book's Amazon page. Click the button that says, "Write a customer review".

Thank you for your support

Made in the USA
Middletown, DE
20 January 2017